D1548516

Lightfoot
If You Could Read His Mind

Lightfoot
If You Could Read His Mind

a biography by
Maynard Collins

DENEAU
1988

Deneau Publishers
760 Bathurst Street
Toronto, Canada
M5S 2R6

Copyright 1988

Book Design: M.J. Hale Graphics
Photo Research and Selection: Cindy Dymond

Printed and bound in Canada

Canadian Cataloguing in Publication Data

Collins, Maynard
Lightfoot

Includes index.
ISBN 0-88879-139-9

1. Lightfoot, Gordon, 1938–   . 2. Singers –
Canada – Biography. I. Title.

ML420.L54c65 1988   784.5′0092′4   c88-094667-9

To Lois, for the reasons only she knows.

Contents

Acknowledgements

Somehow, people don't seem to realize that when they refuse to speak to a writer they have unconsciously confirmed whatever question he was going to ask. Although people accept a "no comment" answer from a politician as an implicit admission of guilt, they somehow feel that they themselves should be freed from the implications of that answer. I'm afraid it doesn't work that way. Subjects of interviews always reveal more than they intend, and questioners always find out more than they ever expected.

Gordon Lightfoot has some very loyal friends. The most loyal ones talk about him freely and try to put the best face on events and actions in the past which, if meanly interpreted, would put him in a bad light. Equally loyal perhaps, but more revealing in their refusal to talk, are those who imperiously demand how you obtained their private phone number and whether the subject of the interview has authorized them to speak about him. Their aggressive silence invokes the image of Lightfoot as some sort of evil Big Daddy figure who would throw them out of the family business and disinherit them in his will if they should dare to talk about him behind his back. Lightfoot himself would be aghast at the image of him being projected by these loyal friends.

Given that both openness and aggressive silence were equally revealing, I would like to thank everyone who contributed material to this book. In Orillia, they included Jay Cody, Bobby Branch, Don Farlinger, Tom Whelan, Phyllis Whelan, Lynn Hamilton, Jim Wood and Carla Palmer. Elsewhere, they included Brita Lightfoot, Fred Lightfoot, Bev Lightfoot, Vic Carpenter, Paul Mills, Terry Whelan, Sylvia Tyson, Elizabeth Moon, Cathy Coonley and others too numerous to mention, some of whom wish to remain unnamed, but to whom I am deeply indebted. Special thanks to Robert and Marlene Markle for dinner, stories and photographs.

I would also like to thank the staff of the Toronto Public Library, the Orillia *Packet and Times*, the Orillia Municipal Hall of Fame, York University Archives, the three Toronto daily newspapers, and the Detroit *News* and Sharon McDonald for the time they cheerfully took to help research articles and photographs; and Baba Torres for her amazing typing skills. Thanks also to the Ontario Arts Council, whose financial assistance is most appreciated.

I am especially grateful to Gordon Lightfoot for the time he made in his hectic schedule to meet with me, to talk freely about his life, and for providing photographs from his personal collection.

Mostly, though, I would extend my sincere gratitude to my editor, Cindy Dymond, who through equal amounts of encouragement and browbeating forced me to stick (more or less) to deadlines, pointed out new areas of fruitful research and helped shape this book into something approaching readability.

Finally, I thank Jacques, Christine and Peter for dragging me, kicking and screaming, into an appreciation of folk and acoustic music when I was much younger and thought that the only music worth considering was rock-n-roll.

Photo Credits

Introduction

A bunch of the lads from up the Ottawa Valley were sitting around the Maple Leaf Hotel not too long ago watching the naked ladies and quaffing a quart or two. When the naked ladies went on their break, the hotel people turned on the giant TV screen. The Ian and Sylvia reunion concert was on. Gordon Lightfoot appeared and sang a song or two. The lads started arguing.

"Jeez, he looks funny," someone said right out loud. "Has he lost a lot of weight or something?"

"Naw, he always looked that way," someone else replied.

"Don't ask me, I never seen him in person before," another interjected. "He don't look like he sounds, eh?"

"What's he singin'? I can't make it out."

"Yeah, I remember that song. I always liked it."

"Hey, remember that song about the railroad?"

"Yeah, that wasn't too shabby. I always liked the one about Gitche Gumee and that boat that sank."

"Gimme a break! Rhymin' gitche gumee and gloomy, you call that a songwriter?"

In the end, nobody ended up watching the Ian and Sylvia reunion (although the general consensus was that Ian had stolen the show). They all ended up arguing about Gordon Lightfoot, until the naked ladies came back.

One guy argued that Gordon Lightfoot was all about railroads and fir trees and northern wastes of wind and snow. Another argued back that he was all about hippies and dope and listening to folk music in some coffeehouse. Yet another said Lightfoot always sang about women who had done him wrong so he was leaving them to go on down the road.

Everybody had an opinion. Nobody said that they had never heard of Gordon Lightfoot.

Everybody knew a little bit about Lightfoot: they had heard his songs on the radio, or their wife had bought some of his albums, or they had read a newspaper article about him not too long ago, only they couldn't remember exactly what the article had said.

For twenty-five years, Lightfoot has been part of Canadian pop music and, for almost two decades, part of America's FM radiowaves. He's been around so long you would think that everybody would know everything about him.

In fact, hardly anyone knows anything about him. He seems to have always been around and yet, like America's Bob Dylan or Canada's Pierre Trudeau, if anyone ever dared say that they really knew what he was all about, you could easily stare him down with a look of disbelief.

His musical career is quickly summed up: he was born in Orillia, Ontario; he became a fixture on the folk music scene of Toronto's Yorkville; his songs were first recorded by Ian and Sylvia and Peter, Paul and Mary; he had a long string of hits in Canada in the sixties, followed by a number of bigger international hits in the seventies; in the eighties, he has developed an increasing social awareness expressed through a number of high-profile public concerts in aid of various relief projects and charitable endeavours, as well as a growing concern with environmental problems; he seems to have been around since Edison invented the phonograph and shows every intention of staying around until the apocalypse.

Lightfoot has managed to stay in the public spotlight without ever revealing very much of himself, except for what he chooses to tell us in his songs. His public utterances are seldom and, when they do come, are short. They are usually part of a public relations campaign to sell a new album or promote another concert tour. After the album is sold, after the tour is over, he disappears from public view one more time.

If his public imagines what he might do when he is out of their sight, they no doubt see him as if in a movie in front of a fireplace scribbling lyrics to love songs late into a cold winter night, the object of his romantic lyrics lying mysteriously desirable on silken sheets just outside of the frame.

His fans would not like their movie to suggest that Lightfoot might be, at heart, a businessman who is ever aware that he is the chief salesman of one product—himself. Nor would they care for a movie scene showing that, in the past, he might have been a coarse and brutal victim of alcoholic over-indulgence. They wouldn't mind a procession of beautiful women who each functioned as his muse, but they would demand that love be the essential foundation of each relationship. The hero of their movie would have to display courage, love and integrity in equal measure. They would probably think that a movie about a ghost in a wishing well—the old-time movie in Lightfoot's own song about himself —would be too fanciful by half.

Life isn't a movie, however. You can't edit out the embarrassing parts, or re-shoot a scene you flubbed. It's done; now you can exult in it or regret it, but there are no re-takes. The following is the way I see the life and career of Gordon Lightfoot. I didn't film the life and I didn't direct it. Perhaps I'm editing the footage to make it seem more logical and tidily manageable than it really was. The close-ups I choose are unlikely to be the ones Lightfoot himself would pick. It does have a great soundtrack, though.

When I look at Lightfoot's life, I see a very Canadian story about a guy from a small town in Ontario who took on the whole world and, by dint of willpower and ceaseless effort, bent it to his demands, even if he had to sacrifice to this successful career a large measure of personal happiness. Like his fans, I see his life in a series of set-pieces acted out in period costume: the child soprano in St. Paul's United Church; the hippie folksinger at the Riverboat; the unfaithful husband and neglectful father; the recipient of yearly adulation at Massey Hall; the troubadour on the road around the world searching for wealth and fame; the lover troubled by the demands of each new love; the voyageur sailing his ship or paddling his canoe on all the lakes and rivers of Canada; the canny overseer of a corporate empire planning the strategy of each new musical move; the father who learns only at his second attempt the meaning of family; the recluse in his Victorian mansion aghast at the demands made of the guy who is, after all, just the product of a small town in Ontario.

The movie isn't over yet. Lightfoot turns fifty this year, and there should be lots of good years in front of him yet, God willing. The age of fifty seems a good time to look back and see what he's done so far in his life. It is not likely that he will once more inspire us with his poetic insight, as he once did in his youth. Aging pop stars do sometimes surprise us with a second wind, though (witness Paul Simon, George Harrison and Robbie Robertson). So, who knows what Lightfoot may yet accomplish?

Of course, nobody can ever hope to read Lightfoot's mind; in his song inviting us to do just that, he was only teasing. In the end, listen to the songs. Play one of his albums and think of Lightfoot as some Don Quixote standing in the rain waiting for a lover who has made unspeakable promises; or as a sailor crossing gale-tossed waters to arrive at the promises of fire-warmth and bed-love in some distant port of call; or as a handsome troubadour waiting below an open window to take a beautiful young woman to some faraway land of song and revelry.

Think of him that way. I'm sure he'll bless you for it.

Chapter 1

Mariposa, a cappella

Gordon Lightfoot grew up in Orillia, Ontario, Canada. Knowing that fact does not lead you to understand all the facets of his character, but without taking Orillia into consideration you probably can't understand anything about him.

Orillia, like Lightfoot himself, is full of contradictions. It is like every other small city in English-speaking Ontario and also totally unlike all others. It is a working-class town with a middle-class sensibility. Its lakefront park is seductively pretty, while its industrial areas further from the lakeshore are depressingly similar to those of a hundred other Ontario towns. Originally built upon the labour of loggers and farmers, it is now best known as a summer resort and tourist area. It boasts a modern town hall and an opera house in a heritage building. A town from which have emerged scholars, artists and politicians of note, it is also the home of the Huronia Regional Centre which, in less enlightened Victorian times, was known bluntly as the Orillia Asylum for Idiots.

If, on a bright summer day, you are travelling the lush countryside of Ontario and decide to visit Orillia, you will learn, by whichever route you take into town, that it is the "Home of Gordon Lightfoot."

You may wish to enter Orillia off Highway 11, the speedy four-lane expressway which skirts the town on its way north, carrying the wealthy lawyers and business executives from Toronto to the rustic luxury of their summer retreats on a hundred different shorelines in the Muskoka Highlands or Lake of Bays or the wilderness of Algonquin Park.

Alternatively, you may wish to take the older road, Highway 12, which crosses the narrows between Lake Couchiching (famed as the occasional site of political conferences which have redefined the direction of the Liberal Party of Canada) and Lake Simcoe (famed for more deadly changes in direction of the winds) and enters Orillia from the east. This highway, which carries the local traffic from the townships hugging the edges of Lake Simcoe, wanders through town, then heads out towards the inlets and islands and rock ledges of Georgian Bay.

On both roads into Orillia, large signs inform you that this is Gordon Lightfoot's home town. The signs fail to inform you that he hasn't lived here in thirty years. Orillians are proud of Gordon Lightfoot.

This is not to say that Orillia had no history before he was born. In fact, Orillia has always been on a major transportation route through Ontario. Since prehistoric times, the site of the town was an important staging point for Indians on the trade route from Lake Ontario and Iroquois country in upstate New York to Georgian Bay, the land of the Hurons. In the seventeenth century, Samuel de Champlain, founder of New France and explorer of much of Eastern Canada and Northern United States, is said to have passed by Orillia and an imposing statue of him now stands in the municipal waterfront park.

The same route became important for the first English settlers leaving muddy York (now the city of Toronto) in the early nineteenth century, as they moved up to the Huron country beyond Lake Simcoe. Settlers travelling to

Georgian Bay would lug their families and goods up the Humber and Holland Rivers, across Lake Simcoe to the narrows, and either turn north through Lake Couchiching and the Severn River or head west from Orillia by the shorter but more difficult route overland to the Coldwater River.

By mid-nineteenth century, Orillia had developed as a small frontier village of about one thousand settlers. It was two days away from Toronto by horseback and was closed to the outside world in winter. Its main streets—Mississaga, Colborne, Matchedash and Coldwater—were laid out in the dirt, but there were stumps in the middle and few boardwalks had been laid for pedestrians. In 1867, the year of Canada's confederation, Orillia was incorporated as a village. Its population stood at some twelve hundred. In 1875, it was officially designated as a town; since 1969 it has been a city, a city which is home to almost twenty-five thousand people.

Nor is Lightfoot Orillia's first citizen to have made good in the world. Orillia's Hall of Fame, housed in its City Hall, boasts a legion of natives who have achieved prominence in national and international affairs: the Honourable Leslie Frost, P.C., C.C., Q.C., LL.D., D.C.L., the Premier of Ontario from 1949 to 1961; Mazo de la Roche, author of the *Whiteoaks of Jalna* series of novels upon which millions of Canadians fed their romantic dreams; Franklin Carmichael, R.C.A., youngest member of the most famous group of painters in Canadian history, the Group of Seven; his fellow artist Lucius Richard O'Brien, founder and first president of the Royal Canadian Academy of Art; Floyd S. Chalmers, businessman, publisher and patron of the arts to generations of Canadian artists through his work with the Toronto Symphony Orchestra, the Canadian Opera Company, the Stratford Shakespearean Festival and the Chalmers Foundation; and, of course, Stephen Butler Leacock.

Leacock wasn't a native Orillian (his family came from Sutton, just on the other side of Lake Simcoe). In 1908, when he was thirty-nine years old, Leacock purchased thirty-three acres of land on a small point on Lake Couchiching outside of town, living and writing there every summer until his death thirty-six years later.

Best known for his thirty-four volumes of humour, Leacock was an eminent scholar of his day, teaching at McGill University and writing, apart from his humorous books, twenty-seven other books of history, criticism, economics, biography and political science.

He called his Orillia property Brewery Bay after the stone ruins of a nearby brewhouse. Each summer morning he would rise at dawn to write for several hours in a study above his boathouse on the lake. The rest of the day he kept for fishing, sailing, raising chickens and tending his garden and farm. In 1925, he tore down the original cottage he had built and replaced it with a large winterized home.

It was at Brewery Bay that Leacock wrote what has been called "the most Canadian book ever written," *Sunshine Sketches of a Little Town.* The little town Leacock immortalized in the book was Orillia, although Leacock called it Mariposa. The sketches were of human foibles, hypocrisies and vanities. At the time, Orillians were not thrilled by the portraits in the book, but time (and death) has erased the wounded pride of those who saw themselves as the life models for the fictional characters of Dean Drone and Judge Pepperleigh and Golgotha Gingham. Today, Leacock's property is a national and provincial historic site maintained by the Leacock Memorial Home Board of Orillia, and is the town's largest tourist attraction. In a reversal of its previous dislike, Orillia now likes to refer to itself as "the sunshine town."

You might think that a town whose reputation is built upon the writing of Canada's most famous humorist would be a cheery sort of place, full of comical characters and exuding a jollity and bonhomie uncommon among towns and cities. Alas, the opposite is true, and Orillia is very much a typical Ontario small town in many ways, bursting with a Protestant work ethic which ensures that everything is neat and tidy, that the people are polite and clean, and that circumspection and self-reliance are the characteristics most highly praised.

Perhaps Hannibal, Missouri, home of Mark Twain, is not a terribly jolly place either. And perhaps out at Uptergrove, not far from town, where the wild Irish Catholics live, there's a lot more fun in the air.

That's not to say that Orillia is not a pleasant place or that the townsfolk are any less than pleasant. In fact, they'll go far out of their way to be nice to a stranger. Orillia is such a typically Protestant place that if you ever wanted to show a Québécois what English-Canadians are like and what makes them different from the Québécois, you couldn't find a better place to take them than to Orillia. The Québécois would find it fascinating and would in no way be disappointed. It would be different, that's all. Like visiting some strange and exotic land.

Dino's Burger Pit on Highway 11 North, Lyn's Deli & Take-out on Colborne Street, the Leacock Memorial Home in Brewery Bay, the Highwayman Inn on Woodside just outside of town, the Orillia Hall of Fame in the foyer of City Hall, Clarkie's restaurant across from the high school on West Street, the boardwalk in Centennial Park—all these help to define life in Ontario in a way impossible to describe to a stranger.

It's a good life, disciplined, hard-working, energetic.

Gordon Meredith Lightfoot was born in Orillia on November 17, 1938, under the astrological sign of Scorpio. He was named Gordon Meredith after his father. Gordon Lightfoot, Sr., had grown up on a farm near Alvinston,

Ontario. His memories of childhood were not pleasant: his mother had died when he was only three, he had been victimized by a stepmother he disliked intensely, and he vividly remembered the tragic childhood death of his sister, who had been burned to death on the family farm when kerosine was being used to destroy potato bugs in the fields.

A former resident of Alvinston many years ago remembers Gordon, Sr., as a pleasant, smiling man who was nick-named "Rosie." She recalls that he took part in amateur theatrics in Alvinston (one of the few forms of entertainment in a small town in the twenties and thirties). He was employed by the Bank of Montreal in Alvinston, but was eventually transferred to the Orillia branch. There he met Jessica ("Jessie") Trill, who could trace her family roots back to the first white child born in Orillia.

It is said that Gordon, Sr., had been going out with an Alvinston girl whom he was expected to marry and that the townsfolk were somewhat shocked when they learned that he had married Jessie.

Although banks no longer exerted quite the authority over their employees' love lives as described by Stephen Leacock in his tale of bank clerk Peter Pupkin in *Sunshine Sketches*, they nevertheless still demanded that bank workers achieve a certain financial stability before marriage was permitted. Presumably, the rule had come into place to lessen temptation to employees who might find the financial demands of a growing family too heavy a burden to cope with honestly.

The Bank of Montreal responded to the hasty marriage by releasing Gordon, Sr., from his job.

There is an Orillia legend that the smiling "Rosie" of Alvinston then became the dour Gordon Lightfoot, Sr., of Orillia, a man who never smiled again. The stern demeanour of Lightfoot, Sr., can perhaps be traced to the fact that his marriage destroyed his bank career, and he was forced to turn to manual labour to support his new family.

Because he was handy with machinery, he obtained employment with Wagg's Laundry of Orillia, where he spent the rest of his working life.

The Lightfoots had two children. Their daughter, Beverley, was the firstborn; then, shortly before the outbreak of World War Two, Gordon was born.

By all accounts, growing up in the surroundings of the Orillia district during the 1940s and 1950s was a fairly idyllic experience. There were, of course, the hardships of wartime and the loss of friends and relatives to the war machine. But, after the war, Ontario entered an unprecedented period of economic prosperity under the guidance of Orillia's native son, Leslie Frost. The people of Ontario were imbued with love and respect for three things: God, the Queen and the Conservative Party. Of these three verities, the death of God came first, the demise of the Conservatives came recently, and the Queen reigns yet.

During this time, Toronto prospered as the manufacturing centre of Canada, Windsor became the car-making headquarters of the country, and the federal government was committed to the ideal of full employment for its citizens. When the soldiers and sailors and airmen returned home, the population of Orillia, like towns and villages everywhere in North America, rose to unprecedented heights.

Gordon Lightfoot, Sr., worked for Wagg's Laundry in Orillia for over thirty years, rising to become manager and providing a modest middle-class income for his family throughout the forties and fifties. As a child, Lightfoot was impressed by how hard his father worked to feed and clothe his family. "I used to see him crawl under one of those great big washing machines," Gordon once said, "and he'd be down there on his back all day because he was the only one

in the place who could fix the thing. It was a hard job."
Lightfoot remembers that making money in those days was
a struggle, but says, "There was always food on the table." It
is obvious that he feels that providing for a family is one of
the essential tests by which a man must be judged. In
Lightfoot's mind, his father passed that test.

Jessie stayed home to keep the house and raise the two
children, Bev and, the apple of her eye, Gordon. In those
days, that was the usual role for a wife and mother, and
Jessie played her part dutifully.

Home was a substantial, two-and-a-half-storey brick
house on charming, tree-lined Harvey Street, close to
school, church and work. An old-fashioned wooden
verandah runs along the front of the house, facing the lilac
trees in the yard. In the back, there is a huge yard with a
garden and lots of trees. A yellow and green clapboard
playhouse, large enough for several children to play inside,
with lots of windows and a steep shingled roof, stands
alongside the house in silent testimony to the remembered
laughter of shouting children during the hot summer days
of childhood. Jessie still lives in her old home today, the
last surviving link between the Lightfoots and the city of
Orillia.

It was Jessie who first noticed that, when Lightfoot was
still a baby, he would hum and sing himself to sleep. By the
time he was around five years old, he could keep a tune. She
encouraged his efforts and continued to help him get ahead
musically through all the days of his youth. The family
remembers such occasions as Gordon standing atop the
kitchen table when still a pre-schooler to sing "Jesus Loves
Me" for his grandmother.

Lightfoot attended West Ward Public School where his
singing talents were further encouraged. In grade four,
Lightfoot made his first record, singing "An Irish Lullaby"
with his sister accompanying him on the piano. The record

was played over the school's P.A. system during Parents' Day at West Ward.

Around this time, he made his first public appearance singing for his mother's ladies club and he also joined the St. Paul's United Church junior choir. The choirmaster, Ray Williams, gave young Lightfoot singing and piano lessons and spotlighted him in the choir as a boy soprano.

Lightfoot was already following in the footsteps of another boy, by the name of Robert Croxall, but known to everyone as Crocky. Three years older than Lightfoot, he had already taken piano lessons and been soloist in the church junior choir. Over the years of their childhood, Crocky would be a role model for Lightfoot. Whatever Crocky accomplished, Lightfoot emulated a few years later until, when both were in high school, they would sing together in the same musical group.

Even at this early age, Lightfoot was becoming something of a child prodigy in Orillia. Orillians still recall his "beautiful soprano voice," which became a town fixture at weddings, civic events and on the radio. Although only a child, Gordon was often paid for his singing. He once joked that he had so many bookings as a child singer, at five dollars a wedding, that he almost had to pay income tax. His repertoire included light opera, hymns, pop songs and classical pieces. His childhood friend Terry Whelan recalls that when Gordon sang The Lord's Prayer in church in his angelic soprano, "people in the congregation would cry, it was so beautiful. Literally cry."

At age twelve, he made a record of himself singing The Lord's Prayer, a copy of which his mother still owns. The next year, he entered the Kiwanis Music Festival held at Massey Hall in Toronto, where he won first place in the Boy's Open Category for Unchanged Voices. That first appearance at Massey Hall singularly impressed the young Lightfoot and, in later years, he would forge a special

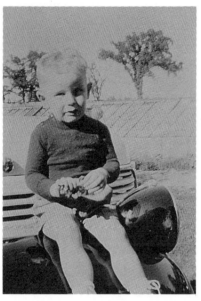

Lightfoot at about age three during a visit with relatives near Alvinston.

Jessie, Gordon, Sr., Bev and Lightfoot, in Orillia around 1944.

Early teens, with catch in hand at Duck Lake.

relationship with the hall, appearing there annually for two decades. In a column he wrote for a Toronto newspaper in 1982, Lightfoot explained, "Massey Hall has always been special to me ... I go way back with Massey Hall, and as long as we're getting along I can't see any reason for leaving it."

The memory of that first musical triumph at Massey Hall remains with Lightfoot to this day. He can still tell you how many contestants there were in his category (thirty), whom he defeated to win the contest (Douglas Hiltz), where his father took him for a celebratory meal (the Severn Hotel outside of Orillia) and what he ate at the meal (frog's legs). The memory of that triumph is probably sweetened by the knowledge that he didn't have to share the victory with anybody else; the prize was his alone, the result of his personal effort.

In September of 1953, Lightfoot followed Crocky into the Orillia District Collegiate Institute (known to students, faculty and alumni as "O.D."). During the fifties, the collegiate taught about one thousand students each year, half of them from town and the others from the outlying rural districts.

High school in the mid-fifties was a world unto itself; a world where the boys carried names like Slats and Nip and Scoot and Rocky and Mouse (all schoolmates of Lightfoot); a world where the girls, who competed for the titles of Miss Holly Hop and Passion Queen, were called Toots and Marg and Toni and Pinky and Marty (also his classmates); a world where the favourite phrases of the day were "Hit it, daddy-o," and "Ain't that a shame," and "I'll never tell," and "Get hip," and "Real cool, man;" a world which revolved around the Key Club and the Keyette Club and the Students' Council and the Glee Club and the Drama Club; a world where the Holly Hop and Twirp Week and the Sadie Hawkins Dance and the Formal Dance and Commencement Day were the social highlights of a school year; a world

where the stars of the school were the members of the
Senior Hockey Team and the Junior Volleyball Team and
the Intercollegiate Football Team and the Six Man Rugby
Team and the Girls' Athletic Association.

North American high school and college students in the
fifties were known as "The Silent Generation." They
sometimes perplexed their elders, who expected them to
exhibit a bit more interest in the world around them and to
generate a little more controversy. (In the sixties, these
same elders would long for the days of the Silent Generation.) Students in the fifties, born just before or during the
Second World War, were the children of the atomic bomb,
and its spectre hung over their silence, even if they had not
yet been given enough information to truly appreciate the
horrifying meaning of nuclear holocaust.

These students didn't eat goldfish or cram themselves
into telephone booths. They listened to rock-n-roll, grew
sideburns, turned their collars up against psychic winds
only they felt, watched James Dean and Natalie Wood at the
drive-in theatres, necked and petted but seldom went "all
the way," and studied enough to make a break from
whatever small towns they were unfortunate enough to be
born in. Noisy and raucous among themselves, to the
outside world they offered only silence. The silence of
indifference, or fear, perhaps.

Into this world of high school sports, clubs and marks
entered young Gordon Lightfoot. He threw himself into
school activities, especially those revolving around music.

Those who remember Lightfoot from his days at O.D.
always seem to recall him in the same terms: he was "shy,"
he was "withdrawn," he was "diffident," rather like his
father.

His father is remembered by some as a surly, withdrawn
man. One man who knew him during all the years he lived
in Orillia remarked that he had never once seen him smile.

Others dismiss his dourness with a shrug, suggesting he was just a regular hard-working guy devoted to his family. Perhaps his unsmiling demeanour merely fit neatly into the serious respectability expected of a businessman and family man in Orillia at that time. And there may be some exaggeration in this description of him, for he certainly was a social person, a member of all the clubs and lodges expected of a businessman in a small town. He was a member of the Masonic Lodge, the Couchiching Golf and Country Club, and the Orillia Curling Club (where he sometimes curled with his son) and he taught Sunday School at St. Paul's United Church, where Lightfoot sang in the junior choir.

Lightfoot himself has retained some of the unsmiling seriousness of his youth, seeming to be excruciatingly shy and fumbling in conversation, an extreme introvert working in a world that prizes exhibitionism and extroversion. And it may be seen as irony that, decades later, when a disease of his facial nerves rendered him unable to smile, he perhaps resembled no one so much as his own father.

Gordon, Sr., was the family disciplinarian. He was not averse to taking the hairbrush to young Gordon when he felt he had done something wrong. Today, Lightfoot realizes there was a battle of wills being played out between himself and his father. He recognizes that his own stubbornness and wilfulness—two traits which have served him well in the music business—were the things his father had tried to beat out of him when he was a child. His father was obviously unsuccessful, for Lightfoot still has incredible reserves of will and stubbornness.

But every male child eventually rises up in rebellion against his father's authority. The family legend about Lightfoot's rebellion is that, sometime around the age of twelve, he took the offending hairbrush (in some stories it is also a strap) and buried it in the backyard, silently announcing that he would stand for no more physical beatings.

Lightfoot now admits that he resented his father for many years and that it was only in his later adult life that he learned to love and respect him anew. When he speaks of his father, it is not to recall hurt and anger, but to reminisce about the fish shacks they built together to go ice fishing on Lake Simcoe.

Perhaps he is more like his father than he cares to admit.

In late 1952, the year before entering high school, Lightfoot joined his first musical group, a barbershop quartet formed by his role model, Crocky. Lightfoot, Wayne Rankin, Paul Lazier and Crocky, all schoolboys, formed The Collegiate Four to take part in a minor competition between a girls' and boys' quartet.

The Collegiate Four played their first gig at the commencement exercises at O.D. in December 1952. The next year, they obtained engagements at local teen dances, at school assemblies, at church meetings, service clubs and other school events.

The quartet joined the Society for the Promotion and Encouragement of Barber Shop Quartet Singing in America Incorporated (SPEBSQSA, for short), travelled to competitions in Midland, Toronto and Sarnia, and won first prize on the CBC television talent contest *Pick the Stars* in the fall of 1953.

By the time the quartet was formed, Lightfoot's voice had dropped from a soprano to a tenor. But his voice would drop even further and, by early 1954, he had to drop out of the Collegiate Four when he could no longer reach the tenor notes. He was immediately replaced by another tenor, Jim Lewis. Later that year, Lightfoot would form another quartet, The Teen-Timers.

When he wasn't singing, Lightfoot became keenly involved in school sports. He and his good friend, Terry

Whelan, joined the school's curling team in 1954. Two years later, the two tried out for the junior football squad. Lightfoot made the team, playing guard. By this time, Lightfoot was fairly stocky and athletic, and he was considered a tough player. In his graduating year, he made the track and field team, where he specialized in shot-putting and pole vaulting. Lightfoot later would claim that he could vault eleven feet and was the school champion, but his old high school yearbooks do not mention such a thing, and his old football coach claims he can't remember Lightfoot ever participating in any school sports. Perhaps that's because, as Lightfoot today remembers, "I was tougher in practice than I was in real games."

During Lightfoot's adolescence the dominant music on the radio and in the jukeboxes was "Hound Dog" and "Peggy Sue" and "Rock Around the Clock," the rock-n-roll which, for a few short years, stood the music industry on its head and shook all the money out of its pockets. The musical heroes of most high-schoolers were Buddy Holly and Elvis Presley and Chuck Berry. At local dances, those who could sing the rock-n-roll and rockabilly sound became the most popular. Local singers like Jack Scott and Jack Bailey and Ronnie Hawkins (originally from Arkansas, but who made a highly successful career move by coming to Toronto) were the most popular on the teen dance and bar circuit.

Lightfoot was seemingly not influenced by any of this at all (he later sneeringly described rock-n-roll as "death after the high school prom" kind of music). He had, in his early teens, two musical passions. The first was jazz. He admired Dave Brubeck and Art Blakey. He gave up his piano lessons for a set of drums, hoping to someday become a cool be-bop jazz drummer. This jazz phase did not last past high school, although there is still a set of old drums out back in his garage. His second love was barbershop and harmony

singing. Although singing barbershop style was a decidedly
uncool thing to do in the mid-fifties, he always seemed to be
able to find three other people to join him in a quartet. The
vocal groups who most influenced the young singers,
according to a former member of one of these quartets,
"were the Four Lads, the Four Aces, the Crewcuts and—the
most jazz-oriented of the lot—the Modernaires."

   After his departure from the Collegiate Four, he set into
motion plans to form a new quartet. By September of 1955,
he had recruited schoolmate Bill Hughes to sing bass, his
friend Terry Whelan to sing lead and classmate Bob
Branch to sing tenor. Lightfoot himself sang his new
musical range of baritone.

   They called themselves the Teen-Timers.

   The group joined the SPEBSQSA and, after three
months of rehearsal, entered the Ontario championships
held in Massey Hall. They finished sixth of fourteen
quartets, a respectable showing for a group so recently
formed and so young.

   During the following school year, they played at every
event at O.D.—the Sadie Hawkins Dance, Commencement, the formal dances and assemblies, as well as at other
social events in Orillia and throughout the area, working
an average of twice a week. Despite the fact that barbershopping might have seemed to be uncool, rock bands of
the time would have killed for such a loaded engagement
schedule.

   Part of the success of the Teen-Timers was due to
Lightfoot's unceasing tirelessness in obtaining bookings for
the band. This single-minded dedication to furthering his
musical efforts was to become a personal trademark throughout Lightfoot's career. Just as important was his dedication
to musical excellence. Displaying another trait which those
who later worked with him would emphasize with admiration, Lightfoot was unrelenting in his demands for perfec-

The Collegiate Four: Wayne Rankin, baritone; Gordon Lightfoot, tenor; Bob Croxall, lead; Paul Lazier, bass.

The Teen-Timers: Gordon Lightfoot, baritone; Terry Whelan, lead; Bobby Branch, tenor; Bill Hughes, bass.

tion in the execution of the music. It was not unusual, when a competition loomed ahead, for the boys to hold long and intense practice sessions four nights a week for the two or three months prior to the event. Another factor was his parents, who helped in any way possible. Gordon, Sr., spent long hours driving the band to its various engagements, and Jessie put her hand to sewing and creating spiffy band uniforms. His father, growing tired of the constant driving, once tried to put an end to it. "So I sat him down—I think it was the first time I ever asserted myself—and I said, 'Look, this is really important,' and I somehow managed to impress it upon him. So he did the driving and everything worked out," he told fellow singer Murray McLauchlan on the CBC radio show *The Entertainers*.

Everyone seems to agree that Jessie helped, cajoled and pushed Gordon forward into the spotlight at every opportunity. Bobby Branch suggests that "there were times when Lightfoot might have quit music" as a teenager, but his mother's encouragement and support kept him at it. Whelan describes Jessie as "somewhat of a stage mother," then adds, "but since then I've seen some real stage mothers who would do anything to push their kids ahead in show business, and she wasn't like that."

Bev, the older sister who would normally have received the most attention in other families, was somehow shunted aside in the family, and Lightfoot agrees that in her youth she was somewhat resentful about all the attention given her younger brother. It is always difficult to be around a star.

Even at this age, Lightfoot's hard work in pursuing his own goals was apparent, as was the presence of others behind the scenes working to help him be successful—two attributes which have contributed in no small way to the furtherance of his long career.

Whatever the reasons, the Teen-Timers prospered.

Numerous "Parades of Harmony" were being held all over Ontario, featuring vocal groups. The Teen-Timers travelled to many of them. In April of 1955, the group entered a contest in Oshawa, a hundred miles away, to choose a group to represent Ontario at an international contest in Miami. The Teen-Timers finished fifth.

That summer, Lightfoot got a job working as a delivery-truck driver for Wagg's Laundry, and Whelan worked for his father's refrigeration company. One of Terry's father's refrigeration customers was the tourist resort called the Muskoka Lodge. With his help, the Teen-Timers got work singing for the guests in the evening. They didn't make a lot of money but the beer was free and the audiences appreciative. As the result of fulsome praise for the group in the Toronto *Telegram*, they were offered a chance to go to New York City to try their hand at recording. After mulling over the possibilities, the group decided, behind the lead of Bill Hughes, that finishing their education was more important. Hughes later attended the University of Toronto and eventually became a professor of philosophy at the University of Guelph. A few years later, Bobby Branch (using the name Bobby Blue) would make it to New York to carve out for himself a successful career as a rock-n-roller in a number of vocal groups.

The following year, the Teen-Timers placed second in the Ontario barbershop championships held in St. Catharines. Terry Whelan insists that they really should have come in first, but that their age was held against them, since the winning group would have to travel around to various conventions and contests to represent the province. "We were so fucking good it was ridiculous," he smiles. Lightfoot disagrees, arguing that the group did not work hard enough to deserve first place and that the Teen-Timers did have flaws, both in song selection and in vocalising.

But it was getting harder to keep the group together. Bob

High School Production of the Mikado. *Lightfoot is standing in centre rear, holding the "Jolly Roger." Crocky squats in front middle, and Sondra Starsmeare is standing far right.*

Robert Croxall (Crocky) at age 18.

GORD LIGHTFOOT

Ambition: Drummer
Prob. Dest.: Diaper wash-
    er at Wagg's
Pastime: Singing
Asset: Loud laugh
Pet Peeve: Squares
Pet Phrase: "Jiggy-vous?"

Branch had quit school and was working in town and Bill Hughes was studying at the University of Toronto. Although the group had hoped to stay together another year and try once more for the Ontario title, the Teen-Timers finally split up after the St. Catharines competition. In retrospect, the group had been extraordinarily successful, especially considering their youth in a musical form dominated by nostalgia and conservatism.

Barbershopping was not Lightfoot's only musical effort in high school. In his tenth grade year, he joined the school glee club, and won a lead part in the Gilbert and Sullivan operetta, *Trial by Jury*, playing the role of the defendant. The following year he played to great success another leading role, that of Ko-Ko the Lord High Executioner, in Gilbert and Sullivan's *Mikado*. Once more Lightfoot was following in the footsteps of Crocky, who earlier had been a star in the school production of *Pirates of Penzance*. A former O.D. student recalls, "In English class we were given the choice of learning some very difficult memory work or appearing in the school's operetta productions." It is small wonder that those with any musical talent at all chose the operettas.

Gordon had an active dating life at O.D., although his only serious relationship was with Shauna Smith, the girl who might, in an idealized way, be the inspiration for the song "Did She Mention My Name?". He was friendly with a number of girls, especially Sondra Starsmeare, the soprano lead in the school musicals.

The summer of 1956, after his grade twelve school year, Lightfoot and Terry Whelan got together and formed a singing duo to appear at the various resorts and lodges around Orillia. For yet another summer, Lightfoot worked driving a truck for Wagg's during the day and sang for the tourists in the evening. Even at this age, Gordon would only sing for money or recognition. Old friends in Orillia recall he would never join in family singalongs or party singing. Music to Lightfoot has always been all work, no play.

One of the people they approached for a job was Jay Cody, manager of the Big Chief Lodge. Today Cody is the executive director and curator of the Stephen Leacock Memorial Home in Brewery Bay, a member of the Orillia Hall of Fame nominating committee, and a tireless booster of civic affairs in Orillia. He remembers Lightfoot and Whelan with a smile.

The Big Chief Lodge catered to about 125 wealthy guests of middle-age, whose main purpose while on holiday was to rest. Normal evening activities consisted of quiet conversation and a couple of rousing rubbers of bridge. Lightfoot and Whelan asked if they might entertain the guests with a few songs on Saturday nights.

Cody offered them a chance, on one stipulation—that their music not interfere with the conversation or the card playing. He was not overly impressed with the duo. He thought that Whelan had the better voice of the two, and that "they were never going to amount to anything anyway." Today, he makes that statement with a rueful grin.

He paid the boys five dollars, to be split between them.

That summer was busy, anyway, as the boys ran from lodge to lodge, playing for little other than beer money (and sometimes only for the beer). It was all part of the plan to gain public recognition. To keep some elements of the Teen-Timers' name alive, they began calling themselves the Two-Timers. Their repertoire consisted largely of calypso music, such as Harry Belafonte's "Jamaican Farewell," and Everly Brothers' songs from the hit parade, like "Bye Bye Love" and "Wake Up Little Susie."

Perhaps it was at this early age that Lightfoot developed his appetite for alcohol, which was years later to wreak havoc on his constitution and his career. Stories abound of

The Two-Timers: Terry Whelan and Lightfoot.
(Photo by James Pauk)

the hi-jinks of the boys, often involving drunken boister-
ousness and falling off docks.

In the fall, Lightfoot returned to O.D. for his grade
thirteen, and Whelan entered grade twelve. Lightfoot
lessened his musical activities but, in compensation, he
began learning how to play guitar. His mother bought him
a twenty-five-dollar Harmony four-string guitar, which he
began fooling around with in his spare time. It would be
years yet before he got himself a real guitar.

During his final year at O.D., Lightfoot and his friends
were devastated by the sudden and unexpected death of
Crocky.

In many ways, Crocky had been a leader of his peers,
achieving all the musical successes in Orillia that Lightfoot
was later to earn. Three years older than Lightfoot, Crocky
had shown the way to use his musical talent to earn respect.
It was Crocky who had first learned to play the piano, been
a soloist in the choir and been a mainstay in operetta
productions, as well as organizing the Collegiate Four
barbershop quartet.

In all respects, Crocky was considered to be a model
member of the Silent Generation. Apart from his musical
activities, he had been a member of the student council and
the school's Key Club (sponsored by the Kiwanis Club). In
1953, he had been elected to the Ontario Boys' Parliament.
In his graduation year, he had won first prize in the school's
annual literary contest with his essay, "Survival of Barba-
rism in Modern Times." Today the essay seems naive and
misinformed, but it no doubt accurately reflects the limited
political and social knowledge of a typical high school
graduate in the fifties. And today, when universities
routinely offer remedial English courses to their freshmen
students, perhaps high school students have even less skill
in essay writing. More ideas, perhaps, less ability to commit
ideas to paper.

When Crocky was growing up, people in Orillia expected him someday to be a successful politician like Leslie Frost. He was the opposite in character of his friend Lightfoot, gregarious to the point of outspokenness (or what passed for outspokenness in the Silent Generation), warm and friendly.

However, during his graduation year, Crocky's father died and Crocky was forced to renounce any ideas of further education in order to get a job. After obtaining his diploma, he looked for steady work. For a short time, he was with C.P. Express before getting a job with a bank in Toronto. In the spring of 1956, Crocky had to leave work because of ill health. He had leukemia.

Within a year, Crocky was dead.

For a teenager, the death of a close friend at such an early age is always a devastating experience, calling into question every aspect of life, often leading to the severest bouts of depression. Perhaps for Lightfoot the death served to strengthen his resolve to make something of his own life as soon as possible; for, soon after Crocky's death, Lightfoot decided to leave Orillia to make his way into the wider world of big city life.

After his own graduation in the spring of 1957, Lightfoot found himself alone. Crocky was dead, Whelan was still in high school, Bill Hughes was away at university, Bobby Branch was working. He had a long summer ahead of him, and whatever he did in the music world would have to be as a soloist.

He tried his hand first at songwriting. In 1957, the current fad was hula-hooping, a craze whereby otherwise sensible people spent hours trying to keep a hoop whirling around their waist by gyrating in a twisting movement. Untold millions of hula hoops were being sold across North America. Contests were held to see who could keep the hoop spinning for the longest time. Teenagers loved to hula hoop to the beat of their favourite rock-n-roll songs.

Despite the fact that Lightfoot was not a fan of rock-n-roll, he thought he had a great idea for a novelty tune and wrote his first song, "The Hula Hoop Song."

He borrowed his father's car and drove to the offices of the song publishing association, BMI, in Toronto, where he pitched the song to Harold Moon, general manager of the association.

Moon was not impressed by the opening lines about a slob who lost his job and spent all his time hula-hooping. Nevertheless, he encouraged Lightfoot to write more material, kindly suggesting he try something "a bit more in the mainstream" of pop music. In later years, Lightfoot cited Moon's early encouragement as a key factor in his success, for it kept his hopes and ideals high at an age when rejection can destroy an adolescent ego.

If the world was not yet ready for the seventeen-year-old Lightfoot as a songwriter, he would just have to get more education in music. Lightfoot was still interested in jazz and had hopes during his senior year in high school to someday make his mark as a jazz drummer. He played the drums in a local dance band, the Charlie Andrews Orchestra. A friend named Buddy Hill was a jazz fan and encouraged Lightfoot's interest to deepen. The two used to read the jazz magazine, *Downbeat*, and in it they noticed an ad for the Westlake School of Modern Music in Los Angeles. The two young jazz fans decided to attend Westlake.

Looking back, Lightfoot describes himself at that time: "When I first started out after high school, no one would have ever thought I could make it. I was clumsy, square, awkward, shy, insecure." He would overcome all the faults he saw in himself in an effort to prove everyone wrong. His musical abilities would be his ticket out of Orillia.

Moving from the small-town environment of Orillia to the sprawling vastness of L.A. was an astonishingly huge step for such a young kid. Let it never be said that Lightfoot has lacked the guts to make a major shift in his life and his career, nor that he lacked the will to carry out major changes. The move to L.A. was perhaps a dramatic gesture to put the provincialism of Orillia behind him and to lessen the hurt at being so alone. But it would involve a drastic change for him. In Orillia he had at least been somewhat of a star. In L.A. he would be merely another of the millions of nobodies.

Still, he entered Westlake, taking courses in piano, orchestration and musical theory. Whatever else happened in his musical career, this formal instruction in music would create a solid foundation.

In 1958, while Lightfoot was attending Westlake, a musical event occurred which was to radically change the course of popular music in North America, and to affect Lightfoot greatly.

Three well-scrubbed collegians named Nick Reynolds, Dave Guard and Bob Shane formed a musical group. The group played neither jazz nor rock-n-roll. It played a new kind of music. They called it folk music. The group named itself the Kingston Trio after the Jamaican capital, in an attempt to identify with the popular calypso music style being sung by Harry Belafonte.

The Kingston Trio did not see themselves as serious music-ologists or as academic collectors of the folk songs of their country. Instead, they perceived themselves as a pop group working within a newly discovered idiom of popular music.

Their first hit record, however, really was an old folk song. Called "The Ballad of Tom Dooley," it had been discovered by folk archivist Frank Warner from the singing of Frank Proffitt, a Carolina farmer who had known the oral tradition of the song for decades. The song told a story of jealousy, murder and retribution by hanging. It was a far cry from the popular rock-n-roll songs of puppy love and teenage romance which ruled the radio airwaves.

"Tom Dooley" was a huge hit and soon there were a
hundred different well-groomed folk groups touring the
college campuses of North America: the Limeliters, the
Brothers Four, the Travellers, the Town Criers, the Jour-
neymen and numerous other trios and quartets of young
men with guitars and double basses, all singing songs of
hoboes wandering America, breakdowns from the Clinch
mountains of Virginia, old Wobbly union songs, Elizabethan ballads of fair maidens and bawdy shepherds, and
more tales of jealousy, murder and retribution.

The folk revival was here. And it was profitable.

Lightfoot was hunkered down at Westlake, learning his
musical theory and his sight reading. The meaning of the
new folk music which was in the air clearly didn't hit him at
this time, since he didn't start singing folk until several years
later. However, Lightfoot was terribly unhappy in Los
Angeles. Perhaps he really was still too much of a hick from
Orillia. L.A. is impossible to navigate without a car. Its air is
unhealthy and dirty. Everyone there is always hustling,
even if they have precious few talents to hustle. Even a kid
with a lot of talent, especially one who is shy or inarticulate,
can easily be overlooked. The music about surfboards and
woodies and hanging five means nothing to a Canadian.
There is an incredible loneliness in being all by yourself in
L.A., unless you're the one being hustled by people who
want something that only you have got.

After only fourteen months of study, Lightfoot returned
to Canada without completing his courses. Buddy Hill, on
the other hand, decided not to return to Canada and never
did. He worked in a number of bands and as a session
musician over the years, and now makes his home in Los
Vegas.

To be sure, what Lightfoot had learned about sight
reading, instrumentation and arranging was to stand him
in good stead when he pursued his musical career in

Canada. He had a new talent which would keep him off the bread line and get him jobs and contracts in the music business.

So, in 1959, Lightfoot left L.A. and began a new phase of his career. He moved to Toronto.

Chapter 2

Hogtown Shuffle

Like some penniless immigrant from abroad, Lightfoot arrived in Toronto in the spring of 1959 with not much more than his suitcase and a few bucks in his jeans pockets. Unlike his experience in L.A., he now had a safety blanket in the fact that Orillia was only ninety miles away.

He had learned a few new skills at Westlake and was determined to make it in Toronto's music scene. In those days, the music scene consisted of rock-n-roll bands in the bars, CBC television on musical variety shows and a few jazz clubs around town.

Lightfoot has always maintained that to become a success in the music business you should shun all other work and concentrate solely on your music. However, when he first arrived in Toronto, he didn't follow his own advice. He installed himself in "Mrs. Smith's boarding house" on Pape Avenue, in Toronto's east end, with an old acquaintance from Orillia, Bren McKinnon. Through his father's intercession with the manager of the Royal Bank in Orillia, Lightfoot got a steady job as a teller in the Royal Bank at Yonge and Eglinton, for forty dollars a week. To help him on his way, his father also bought him a 1953 Pontiac. Unlike his fellow bank clerks, who dreamed only of

someday becoming the president of the Bank of Montreal
or the Canadian Imperial Bank of Commerce, Lightfoot
used his daytime employment to support his nighttime
activities in the world of music.

To most of his fans, Lightfoot has always seemed to be a
laid-back kind of guy, a person who sits and waits for events
to overtake him. In fact, he has always had an incredible
amount of energy and direction, and has been able to
sublimate all aspects of his life to the furtherance of his
career. Ordinary people don't really understand how it
works, but part of any successful show business person's
success is, first, to concentrate every single activity in life
towards becoming successful and, later, to employ others
whose every activity is also devoted to that goal. Even in
high school, Lightfoot had shown glimpses of this dedication and, when he arrived in Toronto, he pursued success
with a single-minded determination and energy.

Working at the bank during the day, he would take any
musical job offered at night. He used every talent he had.
The sight-reading skills he had nurtured at Westlake got
him employment at the CBC as a freelance orchestrator. He
used his singing talent on demonstration records as a
back-up singer. He sang in a musical ensemble called the
Gino Silvi Singers, which worked on television and did
commercial jingles. He used his orchestration knowledge to
arrange and produce jingles. Using the name Charles
Sullivan, he played drums in the Ben McPeek revue at the
King Edward Hotel, called "Up Tempo '60." In a few short
months, he became a whirlwind of activity on the music
scene, seeming to play everywhere at once. It was a crushing
pace for someone also working during the day.

Eventually, he got a break of sorts and got a steady CBC
gig that enabled him to quit his daytime job. He became a
regular on Canada's most popular television program (next
to *Hockey Night in Canada*), *Country Hoedown*. He added

dancing to his talents and became a member of the Singing Swinging Eight.

During the fifties and sixties, *Country Hoedown* was extremely popular in Canada. It starred two singers, Tommy Hunter and Tommy Common (Common left at the end of the fifties), fiddler King Ganam and his western orchestra, comedian Gordie Tapp, the Hames singers, the Singing Swinging Eight, and an assortment of musical guests. It featured a variety of skits, comedy acts and country music. It had a very country, down-home Canadian feel to it. Gordie Tapp was the resident country bumpkin, a role he later reprised in the long-running American country music/comedy series, *Hee Haw*. Nobody in America seemed to notice that his hick farmer character was a quintessential Canadian.

When Lightfoot first appeared on the show, producer Dave Thomas told him, "You're a clumsy son-of-a-bitch, but you've got potential." His potential was evidently fulfilled, for he eventually did 250 shows, sometimes referred to as "the big clumsy, good-looking guy on the end." Tommy Hunter has described the Singing Swinging Eight as "not so much dancers as they were singers who, with some rehearsal, could do a bit of square dancing." Lightfoot says he did every single show filled with dread that he would forget his lines or his dance steps, and he cheerfully admits his faults: "I was an atrocious dancer. Bloody awful. I was the one who was always doin' a do-si-do instead of an allemande left. The only reason they kept me was I was so bloody good at sight reading." His time spent at Westlake was becoming his salvation. He did get a few fans who sometimes wrote to the show asking that Lightfoot be featured in a solo number. The publicity department responded by sending out a glossy of King Ganam. Lightfoot never got his solo.

But he did make a hundred dollars a week, which was a

decent salary for a struggling musician in those days. And he did meet Red Shea, who was later to become Lightfoot's guitar player for many years. Shea was part of *Hoedown*'s Red and Les Trio (Shea, his brother Les, and bass player Bill Gibbs).

The music on *Country Hoedown* held little interest for Lightfoot. In fact, it wasn't really country music at all. Whereas American country music was constantly being redefined by a succession of country stylists—Johnny Cash, Marty Robbins, Waylon Jennings, Willie Nelson, Mel Tillis, and Bill Anderson were all making innovative sounds within the traditions of the genre—the *Country Hoedown* music was stuck in some proto-Canadian time warp. Out on Canada's east coast, fiddler Don Messer was energizing the Maritime folk and country traditions. But, in Toronto, the *Country Hoedown* show seemed to go on forever playing the same old songs the same old way.

In the United States, the folk music scene was changing and becoming ever more exciting. The collegiate sounds of smooth-looking folk groups singing traditionally safe songs were gradually being replaced by solo performers, denim-clad and cowboy-booted, strumming old Martin guitars and singing songs they had written themselves about the events of the day, their voices perhaps whining and their guitars perhaps tuneless, but their protests about the soullessness of America loud and angry.

These singers—Bob Dylan, Phil Ochs, Judy Collins, Joan Baez, Dave Van Ronk, Tom Rush, and a thousand more—came from all the towns of hinterland America. They found a new circuit of concert halls in the coffeehouses which sprang up around and in every college campus in America—the Purple Onion and Gerde's Folk City and the Hungry i, the Mynah Bird and a thousand more.

They weren't really folksingers and they didn't really sing much folk music. They were a bunch of brand new entertainers rejecting both rock-n-roll and jazz and trying to find new styles, sometimes reaching back into folk traditions for melodies and ideas, but not actually taking their music from the people at all. That didn't matter to anybody.

The folk music revival of the late fifties and early sixties was not the first time folk music had been heard in America. The Kingston Trio and Bob Dylan and Joan Baez were following a long tradition.

In the nineteenth century, Professor Francis James Child, a scholar of English literature at Harvard University, had made a landmark collection of oral poetry and balladry, "The English and Scottish Popular Ballads," codifying the 305 folk songs he collected with numbers, so that they were henceforth known to folksingers by his enumeration, such as "Child 9," or "Child 304." Other researchers, such as John A. Lomax and Cecil Sharp, added to the knowledge of folk music. While researching his biography of Abraham Lincoln, Carl Sandberg supported himself by singing folk songs on college campuses, and later published his collection of the best songs, entitled *The American Songbag*.

The Carter Family, Jimmie Rodgers, Woody Guthrie—all sang American folk music in the twenties and thirties and were in turn followed by Pete Seeger, Oscar Brand, John Jacob Niles, Paul Robeson, Sonny Terry and Brownie McGhee, who kept the folk tradition alive during the forties and fifties. Now, they were giving way to a new generation.

There were those in the States (Bob Dylan and Paul Simon, for example) who saw this new folk music as an opportunity to experiment with original forms of self-expression, using quasi-traditional forms of folk styling and melody in a manner as serious as pop music ever gets. There were others, such as Phil Ochs and Joan Baez, who adopted a leftist political stance, using the imagery and forms of traditional folk music to espouse a political agenda, including pacifism and an end to racism.

Then there was the pop music business establishment. They saw the new folk music as merely another product to sell, a new sound to be exploited, a chance at another hit record.

Gordon Lightfoot was just the guy to take advantage of the tension between the different points of view.

There are those who say that Lightfoot's espousal of the genre of folk music was a deliberate career move that had nothing to do with music at all, but rather with doing business. An associate in the late seventies, somewhat disillusioned, said, "If Lightfoot was nineteen today, he'd be making disco music. It's popular and it's safe." There is no doubt a grain of truth in this comment, although another way of looking at it is to say that Lightfoot stumbled around in the darkness for a few years, fooling around with *Country Hoedown* and CBC variety until he found the perfect pop music vehicle for his particular inclinations and talents.

What struck Lightfoot about the new folk music was its relationship to country music: a similar chordal structure, simple enough that almost anybody could play it, but addressing themes in its lyrics beyond the banalities of infidelity and drunkenness. Here was a musical form he could handle instrumentally, at least at a minimal level, and to which he could apply his quasi-poetic songwriting abilities without overreaching the genre. And, what the hell, he might get rich doing it.

It was 1961 and a good time to be in Toronto. Things were changing fast. In music and in literature, the Beatniks who had espoused jazz music and Beat poetry were giving way to a newer generation. All of a sudden, jazz music in Toronto was dead.

For years, jazz had flourished in Toronto in a hundred

different locations, like Barclay's Oasis, the King Edward Hotel, the Colonial (Toronto's first jazz venue), the Town Tavern, the Chelsea, the Left Bank and Larry's Hideaway. In one year, they all closed up or changed music policy. It seemed as if the only jazz club left in town was the venerable after-hours club, the House of Hambourg.

Since 1951, Clement Hambourg had run a succession of jazz after-hours clubs in a variety of locations. He had a series of clubs on Bay Street, Bloor Street and on Grenville. He had hired the best of Toronto's generation of jazz musicians, such as Ed Bickert, Norm Amadio, Moe Koffman and Hagood Hardy. His club had been the meeting-place of artists and intellectuals, like Dennis Burton and Don Francks and Gordon Pinsent.

Now, his was the only club in town.

What was replacing the jazz cellars were the new folk clubs. Two of the earliest on the scene were the Village Corner at 174 Avenue Road and the Clef at 40 Scollard Avenue.

The L-shaped Corner, with its large mural of black slaves being unshackled on its blue walls, was owned by expatriate Britishers, John Morley and Roy Davies. The club, seating sixty people, had a membership list (these really were folk "clubs") of 2,600. During 1960, its most popular performer was Ian Tyson (then twenty-four years old) who performed most Saturday nights.

The Clef was a subterranean room holding about one hundred people. Its mural (all clubs had to have a mural) showed a stylized depiction of the people open-mouthed in song. The Clef, with a membership of nine hundred, had a more pure vision of folk music. Its owner was twenty-one-year-old Peter Ellis, a former factory worker. Winston and Mary Jane Young, who performed traditional material, were the featured performers on Friday nights.

At first, nobody seemed to be sure how to take these new

folk clubs. In a 1960 Toronto *Star* article on folk music, reporter Sid Adilman felt compelled to tell his readers that the Corner was "not a hangout for the student beatnik element or potential lawbreakers. Many professional people belong and sing occasionally." Clearly, something was happening here, but no one was sure what it was.

Downtown, at 7 St. Nicholas Street near Yonge Street, Toronto's most intellectually serious coffeehouse, The Bohemian Embassy, opened for business on June 1, 1961. The Embassy featured both folk music (Bob Dylan played there in 1961 and Ian and Sylvia were regulars) and weekly poetry readings organized by John Robert Colombo (featured poets included Earl Birney, Al Purdy, Milton Acorn, Margaret Atwood and Gwendolyn MacEwan). Don Cullen and five of his CBC friends founded the Embassy, which later achieved notoriety by convincing Bell Canada to list its phone number in the yellow pages under the heading "Consulates and Other Foreign Government Representation."

Lightfoot noted what was happening with folk music all around him and he decided to jump right in.

It was early days yet on the folk music revival scene in Canada. But Lightfoot made a fortuitous decision. When he achieved success a few years later, it was partly because he had a head start on almost everybody and had already become one of the most accomplished writers and singers on the circuit.

He began working up a repertoire of old cowboy songs, hobo songs and songs of love lost and gained. He learned Bob Dylan's "Girl From the North Country," and listened to Ian and Sylvia, who were far more accomplished than he was. He got a few engagements at places like the Orchard Park Tavern and the Village Corner.

He approached his old buddy from Orillia, Terry Whelan, who was now also living in Toronto. How about starting a folk duo? Lightfoot and Whelan had had some good times singing together in the old home town and worked well together.

The Two Tones were born. The name was meant to indicate to an audience that they were a folk duo. Folk duos were becoming very popular in the clubs and coffeehouses which were just beginning to spring up. Apart from Ian and Sylvia, there was Tom and Jerry (in reality, Art Garfunkel and Paul Simon), Jimmy and Jack, and a dozen others. The Two Tones advertised their availability.

If this were the story of anybody other than Gordon Lightfoot, this would be the climax of the story. It has been told a million times or more, about 99 percent of all those who set out to conquer the world. After years of struggle, the hero of the story finally breaks out of the background to make a tiny success in some small part of show business. He gets to play music in public, even gets paid for it. Why, he even makes a record. But sooner or later, the scrounging from gig to gig, the unresponsive audiences, the lure of the whiskey bottle or the needle, all lead to disappointment and disillusionment. That bank clerk's job starts looking really good, at least the money is steady, your employer pays you every two weeks and never tries to rip you off, there's this pension plan which will set you up in your old age. That's somebody else's story. It's not Gordon Lightfoot's.

The Two Tones achieved a modest success. If they were paid less than the most humble lounge pianist reprising "Misty" and "Don't Get Around Much Anymore" in all the bars and saloons of this world, at least they had the satisfaction of knowing they were on the cutting edge of something, a new form of music that appealed to those who thought of themselves as knowledgeable, educated, sophisticated and progressive.

And to tell the truth, Gordie and Terry drank a wee bit. Playing those clubs and bars week after week does that to you. Not a lot, mind you, not like those who could afford the

The Two Tones' album cover and music sheet.

best malt scotches, just draft beer, just enough to keep up with those college kids who saw inebriation as a form of adulthood, just enough so that the shabbiest lounge took on a rosy glow under the dim lights, just enough so that all the women were beautiful at closing time.

And they did put out a couple of records. First they went to New York City and cut four songs, accompanied by two studio guitarists and a bass player, backed up by a trio of female singers. A single, "Lessons in Love," with "Sweet Polly" on the flip side, was released by Quality Records, but it didn't sell very well.

During the summer of 1962, the Two Tones were invited to play at the second annual Mariposa Folk Festival, held in Orillia. The duo had failed to pass the auditions the previous year but in the intervening year Lightfoot and Whelan had improved considerably.

The Mariposa Folk Festival had begun, under the presidency of founder Ruth M. Jones and her husband Dr. F. Crawford Jones of Orillia, in August 1961. Its founding manifesto argued that an annual folk festival was necessary to make it "possible for folksingers to make a career in Canada instead of having first to be recognized in the States. We also want to make the people of Canada familiar with their own folk songs." To achieve this end, each singer was asked to make his repertoire at least 50 percent Canadian content.

The festival ran two days that first year, August 18 and 19, playing to about five thousand people, 90 percent of whom were estimated to be college students. Mariposa was clearly following the example of its model, the Newport Folk Festival in New York State, which had begun in 1959, appealing to large numbers of collegians.

Under the watchful eye of festival producer Ed Cowan and artistic director Ted Schaeffer, the first act to hit the stage on Friday night was Tom Kines, from Ottawa. He was followed by Ian Tyson and Sylvia Fricker (known professionally simply as Ian and Sylvia), the bluegrass group the York County Boys, and fiddler Al Cherney. Jacques Labrecque of Montreal, accompanied by guitarist Marcel Gervais and foot-clogger Aldor Moren, gave the audience a taste of real Québécois singing and dancing. After the concert, the town held a street dance.

The hit of the next day's concerts was the unaccompanied singing of Finvola Redden, a folksinger from Halifax, who sang songs that had been handed down in her family for generations. Fiddler Jean Carignan, The Travellers, Karen James, Bonny Dobson, Allan Mills, Peter Wyborn, Alan MacRae and cowboy singer Merrick Jarrett completed the all-Canadian program.

Although the first festival lost $4,300, it was deemed a great success and everyone looked forward to 1962.

The next year, management of the festival was handed over to Jack Wall, owner of the new Fifth Peg Folk Club in Toronto. He expanded the festival to include concerts for children and workshops for budding musicians. A steam-engine train excursion was organized to run between Toronto and Orillia on the Sunday, which had been added as the festival's third day.

On the opening evening, Ian and Sylvia, Tom Kines, The Travellers, Oscar Brand, Ed McCurdy and the Two Tones appeared on stage. The evening ended with a street dance.

Reviews of the Two Tones were mixed, although two Toronto newspapers spelled the name of the group differently, both incorrectly.

The *Globe and Mail* was negative: "There was a faintly reminiscent flavour of the Kingston Trio when the Tutones (sic), a pair of local boys, came on with Fast Freight, Old Blue, the more familiar Two Brothers, and several other numbers which failed to rouse an expectant audience."

In its roundup of the festival acts, the Toronto *Star* was

more positive, but brief: "The Travellers and the Tu Tones (sic) were great crowd pleasers."

The truth, no doubt, is somewhere in between.

However, with twelve thousand tickets sold and up to ten thousand spectators at Couchiching Beach Park at any one time, trouble was to be expected. There was the incident of the out-house stuffing contest, with the winning team awarded a case of beer. The ban-the-bomb rally didn't please most townspeople. There was a lot of under-age drinking and some festival-goers were accused of "illicit sexual activities."

Townsfolk were fed up with the dirt and the mess and the noise and the drunken hooliganism. One resident near the park set a tire on fire in his backyard, after first carefully checking to see that the winds would carry the smell into the concert area.

The Orillia *Packet and Times* newspaper leaped to the attack: "The festival was attended almost exclusively by young people and, of course, the guitar twanging, the beards, the pseudo folk culture, are merely a peg upon which to hang a weekend of fun .... The elements are all there for converting this folk festival into a riotous nightmare," its editorial thundered. Mayor George McLeod disagreed with the editorial, as no doubt did a number of town merchants who had done a roaring trade during the weekend. But the anti-festival forces were eventually to drive Mariposa from town.

The 1962 festival closed down rather quietly on the Sunday, with Ian and Sylvia singing spirituals at St. Paul's United Church (where Lightfoot had once sang in the choir), the steam engine excursion arriving with much festivity, and a closing barbecue in the evening sponsored by Orillia's Rotary Club.

The Two Tones returned to the clubs and bars of Toronto.

But Lightfoot was no longer content with the Two Tone's career prospects. At the same time as he played with Whelan, he began pushing Gordon Lightfoot, the solo performer. He signed up with a talent agent, Art Snider. Snider was to prove useful to Lightfoot's career, for he knew the booking side of the industry but also, according to Lightfoot, he was willing to give up his performers if they were capable of becoming more successful than he could handle.

Snider became busy on Lightfoot's behalf, arranging a tour for him along with singer Pat Herbey, and sending him to Nashville to record four songs, including Lightfoot's own composition "Remember Me (I'm the One)." The record was released by ABC-Paramount, with the song "Daisy Doo" on the flip side, but it did not see much chart action.

Snider also produced an album by Lightfoot and Whelan, called *Two Tones at the Village Corner*. It was recorded on January 20, 1962 on a stormy Saturday night when Toronto was recovering from an ice storm. It was a live recording of an after-midnight concert by the duo at the Village Corner folk club. Local bass player Howie Morris was added for the recording session. The concept for the album had been borrowed from one American folksingers Bob Gibson and Bob Camp had recorded at the Gate of Horn club in Chicago.

The album contained a dozen songs ranging from calypso to traditional folk material, including several by songwriter Les Pouliot and one cut by Lightfoot, entitled "This is My Song." Luckily it wasn't Lightfoot's only song. The album refused to sell well. Lightfoot began thinking of breaking up his partnership with Whelan, getting the feeling that he was being held back from what he might accomplish as a single act.

Lightfoot still thought of himself as a pop entertainer and was not committed to folk music in any philosophical way, so when Art Snider managed to wrangle him a job in England as host of a television variety show, he leaped at the chance.

Terry Whelan and the Two Tones were history.

Today, Whelan sings part time in a four-person vocal group called the Skylarks, as part of the Tom de Moraes Swing Orchestra. The orchestra does very good versions of the old swing standards, and everyone seems to be having a lot of fun. Whelan says he didn't feel hurt when the Two Tones broke up: "During that whole period, I was teaching school, and we could only get out of town during Christmas, Easter and summer holidays. For Gordie, it was his career. For me, it was a part-time thing. Besides, when we broke up, I could devote myself more seriously to skiing, which I loved but never seemed to find time to do."

When asked if he felt betrayed at the time, he says nothing.

Given Lightfoot's almost painful reticence and lack of congeniality, it seems amazing that any agent could convince Mother BBC that he could handle a job as emcee. As Lightfoot once put it in his inimitable Orillia way, "I couldn't talk for shit."

But, in the summer of 1963, he flew to England and hosted eight television shows of the series *The Country and Western Show*, which insiders referred to as "Rancho Vegas." By all accounts, the program was a seedy affair, featuring live horses and Rodgers-and-Hart, Oklahoma-style musical production numbers, a large orchestra and Broadway-style sets. It was Americana, British-style. While Lightfoot completed his assignment without incident and was not fired, neither was he offered more work.

There is no evidence that, while in England, Lightfoot was influenced by any of the truly revolutionary musical experiments happening there at the time. Beatlemania was sweeping England, even if it had not yet made its way to

The Two Tones:
Terry Whelan
and Lightfoot.

(Photo by Herb Nott, courtesy of Lightfoot)

Lightfoot's first promotional shot as a solo, taken at Rouge Hill in 1961.

North America. The British pop charts featured for the first time the songs of home-grown British talent. The clubs around London featured a host of new pop groups, all pulsating to the Merseybeat sounds of the Searchers or Cilla Black or Rory Storm and the Hurricanes, or else to the rhythm-n-blues beat of the Rolling Stones and the Kinks and the Animals and the Bluesbreakers. On Carnaby Street, a revolution in fashion was underway, led by designer Mary Quant and a skinny model named Twiggy.

Perhaps Lightfoot missed all of this because he had recently married. He had met his new wife, a beautiful blonde Swede named Brita Olaisson, back in Toronto. When his roommate Bren McKinnon had left Mrs. Smith's to move in with a new girlfriend, Lightfoot had made a series of moves before finding a nice room in a boarding-house at 161 Admiral Road in "the Annex," just across Bloor Street from the University campus in mid-Toronto— a neighbourhood of tree-lined streets and large, comfort-able red brick houses, some owned by well-off single families and others used as boardinghouses for students and singles. Brita was already a tenant there.

Brita had come to Canada in an effort to improve her English. She did some publicity work for various Swedish enterprises, including promotion of boxer Ingemar Johann-son. Johannson, who called his fists "toonder and light-ning," became the world champion heavyweight for exactly one fight. He defeated champion Floyd Patterson in 1960 to win the title, but then a year later lost the rematch to Patterson, as well as the subsequent rubber match. Apart from her promotion work, Brita also worked as secretary for the M.P Hofsteder Company, which sold Swedish bookkeeping machines.

Brita came from a poor Swedish family, but she had resolved to make her way upwards in the world by her combination of beauty and brains. Before coming to

Canada, she had worked as an organizer for the Swedish Conservative Party and as an organizer of trade exhibits throughout Sweden. Raised in the working-class Sodermaln district of Stockholm, from which Greta Garbo had emerged to find world-wide fame two generations earlier, Brita was a bright, determined young lady eager to escape from poverty.

The summer of 1961 when she arrived in Toronto was a sweltering one. On the third floor of the Admiral Road boardinghouse, Brita found the only available relief from the heat wave was the cold water of the bathtub in the shared third-floor washroom, where she spent many sweltering hours.

Brita well remembers meeting Lightfoot that hot August of 1961. She was immediately attracted by his youthful good looks and he was obviously stricken by her icy nordic beauty.

Everyone who has met Brita describes her in almost identical words: she was "that beautiful blonde Swedish woman," a phrase uttered by the men who knew her in a whisper of awe, almost. It does not seem any wonder that the young Lightfoot was stricken by the beauty and sophistication of the world traveller three years his senior.

The two fell madly in love and began an affair which lasted until late in 1962 when Brita announced she was returning to Sweden. She left Canada, taking a ten-day ocean voyage across the stormy winter Atlantic.

Lightfoot obviously missed Brita desperately, for he immediately called her in Sweden. According to Brita, she had not been home more than a half hour when Lightfoot was on the phone proposing marriage. She accepted his proposal and the wedding date was set for April 6, 1963.

Lightfoot came to Stockholm, where they were married. They took a week-long skiing honeymoon in Lilliehammer, Norway.

Brita and Lightfoot at their wedding in Stockholm, April 6, 1963.

The newlyweds at Blarney Castle, Ireland.

Immediately after the honeymoon, Lightfoot brought Brita to England, where Snider had obtained the BBC television work for him. They stayed in England for five months.

The honeymoon was hardly over when Jessie came over from Orillia to stay with the young married couple. In hindsight, it seems to have been an insensitive act, one for which Brita has never forgiven her former mother-in-law. The newlyweds barely had time to set up housekeeping when the first of many resentments and disagreements between the couple interfered with their happiness.

While living in England—and, perhaps, because of his marriage—Lightfoot suddenly found himself writing reams of new material. By the time he and Brita returned to Canada in the fall of 1963 he had more than thirty new songs in his portfolio.

If the London which Lightfoot had hardly noticed was swinging, the Toronto he returned to late in 1963 was sizzling. It seemed that in every basement there was a new folk group or rock-n-roll band practising to emerge into the bars and clubs and dances and hootenannies, conquer the world, create a revolutionary new music and make a million dollars. There was lots of work around.

Apart from the Embassy and the Clef and the Corner, there now was added the Purple Onion, the Village Gate, the Fifth Peg (owned by Jack Wall, who was also running the Mariposa Folk Festival), the Gates of Cleve, the Cellar, and a host of others.

The Lightfoots found a small basement apartment on Arlington Avenue in west-central Toronto. Brita was by now pregnant and Lightfoot had to make some money. Luckily, it was a good time to make money in Toronto.

He turned once more to folk music. He listened to and copied from the albums of Bob Dylan who was, by this time, becoming the rising star in the New York folk music scene.

He trudged from club to club, listening to what all the other folkies were doing. He continued writing new songs and built himself a repertoire of folk material.

Then he hit the road. He played a thousand different bars and clubs in and around Toronto and anywhere else he could get booked. He worked hard, but for little money. By the time his first child, Fred, was born on February 1, 1964, he was still earning around a hundred dollars a week. When he was working. It was a rough life.

While Lightfoot was out singing at night, Brita was in the basement apartment, looking after her baby. It would not be long before an irreparable rift appeared in their marriage.

As he made the rounds of the clubs, Lightfoot was developing a small but rabid following of folk fanatics who would go to hear him in every club. And he was making a lot of new friends. Unfortunately for Brita, a lot of his new friends were women. But there were others, such as Ian Tyson and Sylvia Fricker.

Ian and Sylvia had first joined forces as a folk duo in the fall of 1959 and, since then, had become among the most professional singers in Toronto. Lightfoot had first seen them at the Corner, where Tyson had a steady Saturday night gig and where he alternated sets with Sylvia.

Lightfoot had been mightily impressed by their professionalism and stage presence as early as 1961. Many years later, he admitted, "When I saw that combination of folk and country music, I knew what it was I had been looking for. It was like seeing the light of day." The particular song which influenced him greatly was "Dark as a Dungeon," a regular part of Ian and Sylvia's act, and which the Two Tones had included on their live album.

Lightfoot struck up a friendship with the Tysons. Ian and Sylvia were not the only husband-and-wife folk duo making the rounds of the coffeehouses and folk clubs (Joni and

Fred at about age six, with his father.

*The Lightfoot home
at 222 Blythwood,
in Toronto.*

Chuck Mitchell worked out of Detroit, and Jim Kweskin and his wife Maria Muldaur were the integral part of the Jim Kweskin Jug Band), but they seemed to exemplify the joys of working and sleeping together. Unfortunately, Lightfoot was never able to find such an arrangement in his own life.

Ian Tyson thought Lightfoot was a woefully inadequate guitar player (he might have known all of six chords and a few variations then), so he took it upon himself to teach him. They spent long hours together, working very hard, trading songs, listening to Dylan, Woody Guthrie and the Carter Family.

Lightfoot was a fast learner. The effect of upgrading his guitar technique was revealed in his improved songwriting. One disadvantage of being a composer-performer is that, as a composer, you must always restrict yourself to writing what the performer side of yourself is able to perform. Lightfoot had always had a reasonably pleasant voice with adequate range. Now, with Tyson's help to improve his guitar playing, he was able to stretch his songwriting to new limits. It showed in his performances.

While he was in Europe, Lightfoot had missed the 1963 Mariposa Folk Festival. It was just as well. Orillia had a new mayor, J.C. McDonald, who did not support the festival and, despite the professionalism of the folk acts, the problems of crowd control of the seventeen thousand patrons overcame the organizers.

Although the festival attenders had been banished to the Silversleeve Park at Severn Bridge, fifteen miles north of Orillia, and bussed to the various events, Police Chief W. E. McIntyre claimed after the festival that the hooligans in the crowd "gave Orillia the worst 48 hours in its history." The town vowed that the festival would never again be held in, or near, Orillia.

After protracted legal battles, which the festival lost, the

1964 festival was, in the end, held at Maple Leaf Stadium on Lake Shore Boulevard in Toronto. Despite the presence of Lightfoot, Buffy Sainte-Marie, the Reverend Gary Davis and all the stars of folk music, the festival lost five thousand dollars. The Mariposa Folk Festival was in deep trouble.

(Apparently someone forgot to inform headliners Sonny Terry and Brownie McGhee that the festival had been moved from Orillia to Toronto, for they never showed up.)

During the winter of 1964–65, Lightfoot had a more-or-less steady gig at Steele's Tavern on Yonge Street. It was mostly a drinking crowd at Steele's, so not a lot was expected of the performer. It was almost like being paid to practise and rehearse. Old friends dropped in. Steele's was about as close as a tavern could get to the special relationship between the audience and the performer found in a folk club. A lot of pickin', a lot of singin', a lot of drinkin'. Man's work.

Steele's Tavern was owned by Steele Basil, a Greek immigrant who had come to Canada in 1923 as a teenager and who had rented a restaurant on Yonge Street in 1936. In 1950, after he had obtained a liquor licence, he bought the entire building and put in a lounge upstairs. In 1959, he enlarged the lounge to hold 180 patrons and began a policy of featuring folk music. One of the first performers he ever hired was Lightfoot and he had given him work ever since. According to Basil, "Lightfoot played over thirty engagements here during the first three years and when he was not known. But then he became a star and I couldn't afford him anymore."

Today, Brita claims that her marriage was still intact and happy at this time, but Lightfoot recalls differently. In a recent interview for *Canadian Composer* magazine, he said, "Pop Steele would sit me down in his office—I was having my first bout of marital problems at the time—and he'd advise me."

Steele's was known as the watering hole of Ryerson, after the drinking habits of the students of Ryerson Polytechnical Institute, a community college just around the corner. Located between two large record stores, A&A's and Sam's, Steele's was one of the very few taverns featuring folk music. This was partly due to Steele's preference for quiet music and partly due to his search for a music policy to set his tavern apart from all the others featuring country music, rock-n-roll or strippers.

Looking "like a clean-cut version of King Ganam," as he was described at the time, Lightfoot performed a few of his new compositions, such as "Silver Grey Silver Cloud Talking' Rolls Royce Blues" (a humorous description of the time rockabilly singer Ronnie Hawkins decided to buy a Rolls Royce and shocked the salesman by kicking the tires and asking for a test spin around the block), as well as such folk songs as "The Jolly Tinker" and "Wabash Cannonball," Leroy Van Dyke's country song, "The Auctioneer," and Dylan songs, such as "Talkin' World War III Blues." He was working on his chops, perfecting his craft.

Ian and Sylvia were frequent visitors to Steele's and were particularly intrigued by the new compositions Lightfoot was slipping into his sets. The rowdy audience at Steele's loved the old folk and country favourites and Lightfoot supplied their insatiable demand. But every once in a while he would mumble that the next song was one he had written himself and he would launch into one of his new songs, like "For Lovin' Me." Ian and Sylvia were impressed.

Part of Ian and Sylvia's success as contemporary folksingers was due to Ian's ability to write a new song that sounded as if it might have been written thirty years before by a Depression-era hobo resting before he caught the next freight to Vancouver or to California or to Mexico. Mixing the imagery of the drifter, the contemporary cowboy and a Promised Land somewhere down the road, Tyson created contemporary, but timeless, songs which, if they did not really spring from the people, sounded as if they had.

Lightfoot, too, was even then capable of catching the perfect turn of phase to illustrate a romantic yearning for the rural past while acknowledging the urban present. In his song, "Early Morning Rain," he wrote what is perhaps the most perfect one-liner illustrating the difference between the dust-bowl folksingers of the thirties and the new generation of folkies of the sixties: "You can't catch a jet plane/Like you can a freight train." That phrase, and the rest of the song, sent shivers up the spine of Sylvia Tyson. Here was a gifted new songwriter. And nobody had even heard of him yet.

Bob Dylan has always said that he wished he had written "For Lovin' Me" and there is no doubt that there is a Dylan influence in the song. To be sure, like the Rolling Stones' "Under My Thumb" and Dylan's own "Don't Think Twice (It's All Right)," the song contains more than a trace of a misogynist theme that Lightfoot's female fans either ignored or accepted as part of the whole package.

Critics and fans might have done well to pick up this early indication of misogyny for it has never completely left Lightfoot's work; and his tortured relationships with the various women in his life seem to indicate that these songs were indeed revealing the true nature of the writer. In seeming contrast, Lightfoot has also written sensitive love lyrics which stand in opposition to the disdain and contempt towards the female sex contained in these lyrics.

It is probably fair to say that the anomaly between the misogynist lyrics and the romantic lyrics accurately reflects the duality in Lightfoot's own relationships with women, relationships which veer from intense love to extreme bitterness and are often teetering on the balance between the two extremes. However, it is easier to criticize relationships from without; Brita, who inspired lyrics of both love and pain, had to live with the duality every day. She was the one in the basement apartment with baby Fred while Lightfoot was out in the clubs, singing, laughing and entertaining.

Ian and Sylvia asked Lightfoot if they could include "Early Morning Rain" and "For Lovin' Me" on their next album. Who would say no? In the event, the Tysons went even further, naming their 1965 album *Early Morning Rain* and giving Lightfoot's song more international exposure than a tavern singer dare even dream of. Adopting a fatherly attitude, Ian Tyson redoubled his efforts to give Lightfoot a leg up in what was fast becoming the cutthroat world of folk music.

Ian and Sylvia were managed by Albert Grossman, the bearded, long-haired, greying mentor to Bob Dylan, Peter, Paul and Mary and other folk acts. He was a power to be reckoned with, both in the United States and in Canada, perhaps *the* power. He was the behind-the-scene professional all folkies needed to guide their careers.

Grossman was known in the industry as "God," a reference to the fact that he had created the folk group Peter, Paul and Mary. After the initial success of the Kingston Trio in 1958, Grossman, then the Chicago-based manager of folksinger Odetta, began to cast around to manufacture another folk trio. From the first, he wanted a woman to anchor the group. After watching other folk acts and searching Greenwich Village, he found the three he wanted: tenor Peter Yarrow, the attractive blonde Mary Travers, and Noel Stookey, a Greenwich Village regular. Noel became Paul, and the group was born under the guidance of musical director Milt Okun, who had previously worked with The Brothers Four and the Chad Mitchell Trio.

Despite the fact that Peter, Paul and Mary was a manufactured group (much like the Monkees, later), they immediately became a popular success and even a critical success,

due partly to Mary Travers' well-known leftist politics.
They introduced the songs of the new, young songwriters,
such as Dylan's "Blowin' in the Wind" and, later, Lightfoot's
"For Lovin' Me."

Since the early-sixties folk music scene was, in part, a
deliberate rejection of, and rebellion against, the teen-angst
excesses of most current popular music, folksingers cultivated an image of studied unprofessionalism in presentation and stage mannerisms that implied a one-of-the-gang
relationship with the audience.

In truth, most folksingers were better educated and more
middle class than their image implied. But, if they were to
play the man-of-the-people role, they needed an Albert
Grossman behind the scene, a shark to swim amongst the
other sharks in the murky waters of business, contracts and
deals.

Ian brought Grossman's partner, John Court, to Steele's
Tavern to hear Lightfoot. It was an incredibly generous act
by Tyson. Whereas a short time earlier there had been only
a few folk acts in Canada, the field was now getting more
and more crowded. Getting someone else started would not
have been a priority to most other singers. Ian shrugged.
He was so confident in his own abilities that jealousy of a
raw newcomer was foreign to him. Sylvia felt it was in the
best interests of everybody to create a distinct Canadian
generation of singers and composers who could all rise to
the top together.

"The music scene was amiable then, not cutthroat like
today," she recalls.

Today, such an attitude would probably be considered
anti-American, anti-free trade, naive, even. But, in truth,
such a thing actually happened, even if nobody much
noticed it at the time. If Dylan eventually became the king
of the folkies, the court was full of Canadians, including Ian
and Sylvia and Lightfoot, but also Neil Young, Joni

Mitchell, Leonard Cohen, The Band and parts of Buffalo Springfield. Most of these people moved to the States and became part of the American scene. Ian and Sylvia didn't. Nor did Lightfoot.

John Court liked what he heard. Privately, he was worried about Lightfoot's lack of dynamism on stage but he thought that, with more experience, Lightfoot could develop into an exciting performer. That was one prediction that never came true.

If Court had troubles with Lightfoot as a performer, he had no doubts that he could be a successful recording artist. He advised Grossman to sign him up, even offering to produce Lightfoot's first album.

Lightfoot was coming highly recommended, so Grossman wrote up a management contract. Lightfoot eagerly signed.

Now, finally, he was on the verge of making it. If, to his public, it looked like he was an overnight success, Lightfoot knew this was the culmination of his eight-year-long odyssey. His songs were soon to be released on Ian and Sylvia's album, which was sure to be a bestseller. He had the best manager in the business. He was going to make his own album in the near future. He had a small group of dedicated fans all over the city. He smiled a lot. Not bad for a kid from Orillia.

All around him, the folk music world was exploding. It seemed that on every college campus a new coffeehouse was springing up. On every corner in the part of Toronto called Yorkville, a new folk music club was opening. And Lightfoot was right in the middle of things.

Economics was a large part of the explosion. Any empty room anywhere could become a folk club. You didn't need a liquor licence, since booze was not part of the scene. Kitchens were not an absolute necessity and, when they existed, tended towards the simple. The folksingers them-

Ian and Sylvia, April 1964.

At Steeles Tavern about 1962.

selves worked for a relative pittance, often accepting a humble room and board in lieu of cash. Lightfoot himself was to be the first to demand lots of money for an appearance but, for the moment, anyone with a couple of hundred bucks to speculate with could get into the folk music coffeehouse business.

There was the Village Corner and the Purple Onion and the Gates of Cleve and Hills Corner Club and a dozen other little places on the campuses of the University of Toronto and the newly established York University and around the Ontario Teachers' College.

The success of the Purple Onion was a typical story. Begun in 1961 by a group of five accounting students (soon reduced to four: Sam Gutmacher, Barry Witkin, Al Tylel and Al Lastman, brother of Mel who is now mayor of North York) who each had invested two hundred dollars, the Onion, located on Avenue Road near Bloor Street, had a membership list of thirty thousand (at fifty cents per card) within three years. In 1963, it was the most financially successful folk club in the city, partly due to the owners' astuteness in finding up-and-coming talent before it was priced out of the coffeehouse market. The one mistake the group made was in turning down Peter, Paul and Mary early in the club's history, because the asking price of $350 a week seemed too steep.

As an emerging local star, Lightfoot could always get gigs in Toronto. It was up to Grossman to get him work in the United States and in the rest of Canada.

He was still in love with Brita. It was just that a wife and family didn't seem to really fit in with all the rest of the things that were happening to him.

Chapter 3

Struttin' in Yorkville

It was a cold and bitter November in 1964 when Lightfoot boarded the Trans-Canada Airlines flight to New York City. Grossman had been true to his word, and Lightfoot was off to record his first solo album. Grossman's associate, John Court, was producing the session.

In years to come, Lightfoot would be met at every airport by a stretch limousine half a block long, but this first time he had to be content with a yellow Checker cab. New York wasn't Toronto and nobody knew who he was. The assistant engineer, whose job was to keep the studio log detailing the singers, instrumentation and songs, didn't know him and apparently didn't care. An older man who had no interest in folk music at all, he listed the singer as "Gordon Whitefoot" on his log.

If the Studio D of one of New York's many recording companies had the look and feel of the big time, it was the look of grey walls and the feel of a "cold and angular atmosphere," according to producer John Court.

The first song recorded was Lightfoot's "Rich Man's Spiritual," which that same assistant engineer listed as "Richman's spiritual" on his take sheet, as if it was a song about or by some fellow named Gordie Richman or something. Lightfoot was quickly learning about the cold impersonality of New York.

"Rich Man's Spiritual" may have had its roots in the junior choir of St. Paul's United Church in Orillia but, if so, it was also a sly and clever satire about Protestantism, about what Pierre Berton has named "the comfortable pew." The song describes heaven in terms of what the wealthy on earth might expect upon arriving: a long white robe, slippers of gold, wings of silver. At the end of the song, the rich man realizes he also needs a "poor man's trouble" (which he never had in life) in order for the smiling angel to lead him into heaven.

In a couple of days thirteen other songs had been recorded. Over the sessions, the atmosphere softened as the staff realized that the album being recorded was different from anything they had ever heard before. The songs included "The Way I Feel," (like a robin whose babes have flown to come no more), "For Lovin' Me" which was to become a hit for Peter, Paul and Mary later that year (the French version they sang was called "Tu n'aurais jamais du m'aimer"), "Early Morning Rain" (already a hit for Ian and Sylvia), "Steel Rail Blues" (later to be a hit for George Hamilton IV), "I'm Not Sayin'" (a Lightfoot hit single), and "Ribbon of Darkness" (soon to be a Number One country hit for Marty Robbins).

The album included five other Lightfoot compositions, along with Ewan McColl's folk standard "The First Time (Ever I Saw Your Face)" which was an ever-present part of wedding ceremonies in the sixties, Phil Och's arguably best song, "Changes," and Hamilton Camp's apocalyptic hymn, "Pride of Man."

At the end of the recording session, Lightfoot, Grossman, Court and the accompanying musicians, David Rea, Bruce Langhorne and Bill Lee, were all pleased, for it had the sound of a hit album. Indeed, the album was to generate five hit singles, an achievement on a level with albums by the Beatles.

After the recording session, Lightfoot returned to Toronto. Once an album is recorded, there is a lag time—often incredibly long—before the record is finally available in the record stores. Back in Toronto, nothing had changed, really, so he fell back into the groove of playing clubs and hanging around with musician friends.

He huddled down in the basement apartment with Brita and Fred, hopeful that 1965 was going to be a whole lot better. It was a frustrating period. Perhaps success would be just around the next corner, but in the meantime there were bills to be paid, food to be bought and diapers to be washed. Lightfoot and Brita were fighting a lot.

Lightfoot was getting a lot of club work but he was also doing a lot of partying. And all that money spent on carousing came out of the family budget. Brita would try to get a babysitter and come to the clubs once in a while, but never did she really feel welcome. The marriage, after only one year, was already showing signs of strain.

But Lightfoot was right about his career. Everything was going to change. The year 1965 was to be the year of Gordon Lightfoot, the year when nobody in the country could turn on the radio without hearing a Lightfoot song, when nobody could turn on their television without seeing him perched upon a stool and strumming his guitar, when nobody could read a newspaper or a magazine without reading another story about folksinger Gordon Lightfoot.

In 1965, Lightfoot should have been a very happy man.

In the United States, Grossman's organization went into full gear, looking for a record company to release Lightfoot's album and making every attempt to place his songs with other singers. They were successful on all fronts.

After a proposed deal with Warner Brothers records collapsed, the United Artists label paid a hefty advance to

Peter, Paul and Mary in Toronto, February, 1962.

Lightfoot in his basement apartment on Arlington Avenue in Toronto, 1965.

put out the album. Within a couple of months, both Peter, Paul and Mary and Johnny Cash had recorded "For Lovin' Me." The Peter, Paul and Mary version became a hot single, flying to the top of the charts. Marty Robbins' version of "Ribbon of Darkness" topped the country charts. Both the album and single of *Early Morning Rain* recorded by Ian and Sylvia became bestsellers.

In the blink of an eye, Lightfoot was a major international songwriting success. The royalties starting rolling in. He was becoming rich.

And almost nobody in the general public had ever heard of him.

But Lightfoot is nothing if not lucky. Another piece of the puzzle of fame and stardom was about to be put into place.

Bernie Fiedler, a Toronto entrepreneur and music promoter, had come up with a great idea. He and his wife, Patti, ran a small folk club called the Mousehole, and now he was going to open the greatest coffeehouse of them all, in the centre of Yorkville. It was going to be not only a club, but one that harkened back to the great days of the show boats which plied the rivers and lakes of Canada and the States at the turn of the century. He would call it the Riverboat.

The Riverboat really did look like a boat on the inside, with netting on the wall, tongue-and-grove pine walls, brass portholes and nautical themes wherever you turned.

It became a gigantic success.

Fiedler started bugging Lightfoot to play at the Riverboat. But Lightfoot and Grossman had devised a new strategy to further Lightfoot's career. His asking price for a gig was now one thousand dollars a week, a huge jump from the hundred a week he had been earning until now.

A thousand a week was an astronomical sum for a single performer in those days. There wasn't one club in the whole country that paid that kind of money. There were a few clubs in the States that were used to that kind of salary demand, but none in Canada.

However, there was one hitch to their plan. Lightfoot couldn't immediately get a green card, the permission of United States immigration to work in that country. So, Lightfoot was in a dilemma. He had named his price, but there was nobody around who could afford to pay it.

Lightfoot stuck to his principles and went into a self-imposed performance holiday.

He continued as before, sitting around writing new songs, drinking with his buddies, waiting for the next gig. Some things had changed, however. The royalties were starting to flow in, and day-to-day life became a little easier.

The only trouble was Lightfoot wasn't playing anywhere.

Finally, in June, Fiedler broke down and agreed to pay Lightfoot's salary if Lightfoot would play four sets a night. He figured that, by turning his audience out after every set, he might not lose too much money. To hedge his bet, he optioned several repeat engagements. Sooner or later, he reasoned, Lightfoot would jam the Riverboat for every set and he'd then make up any money he had lost during the first week.

The Riverboat had immediately become the most important and most successful folk club in Canada. For his part, Lightfoot achieved another success totally on his own terms: he was getting the gig at the Riverboat and also getting his price.

But Fiedler had made a good deal as well. From the first, Lightfoot packed the Riverboat and his successive appearances brought in more and more customers until the club, permitted by fire regulations to hold only one hundred and twenty people, often was packed with upwards of two hundred enthusiastic Lightfoot fans.

The Riverboat was the perfect setting for the intimacy of

Robert Markle, 1967.

Bernie Fiedler, with patrons inside the Riverboat.

Lightfoot's material. From the first time he strode onto the small stage, he felt that this was what the long struggle had been about.

The Riverboat customers were a discerning crowd. They were devotees of a particular type of music and the Riverboat provided the best of the folk genre to them: Phil Ochs, Richie Havens, Ian and Sylvia, Kris Kristofferson, Bruce Cockburn and everybody, in fact, except the acknowledged master of the art, Bob Dylan.

Seizing the moment, Lightfoot became the most successful entertainer of the lot. Visual artist Robert Markle described those hot summer nights in 1965: "Beards, businessmen, lovers, turtlenecks, sweaters straining, mini-skirts, net stockings, leather boots, vinyl thighs, and electricity, high heels, bell bottoms, crossed legs, wide eyed attention, now rapture, all that audience, teeny boppers allowance spent, sweet girls, college students, fans, all there, devouring this man, love eyes looking, love ears leaning forward to listen."

By 1967, when the national media in America discovered the Summer of Love, all the best things about what became known as the hippie way of life had already passed. It was a short, gentle and impossible way of life, fuelled by hope, generosity, pacifism and, ultimately, dope. By the time self-serving relief groups, such as the Diggers, were required to organize food relief for the thousands of young people with no visible means of support, and no intention of finding any soon, any attempt to seriously arrange a non-capitalistic, alternate form of communal living was doomed.

But in the summer of 1965, at the Riverboat Club, in Toronto's Yorkville, it sometimes really looked as if the millennium had arrived. It appeared as if the longings, fuelled by the sweet smell of marijuana, for a way out of the middle-class treadmill of psychic failure were being fulfilled. Nobody dared mention that a thousand dope dealers, a bunch of record companies, a hundred manufacturers of tacky beads, T-shirts and hookah pipes, Bernie Fiedler, and

Gordon Lightfoot (at a grand a pop) were all making money out of young people's legitimate aspirations to discover an alternative to the desperation of the lives lived by their families.

Then there was the sex thing. Oh, yes, to understand Lightfoot's love life—and the love lives of almost everybody in the crazy mixed-up world of pop music—you must remember how much of that mid-sixties hippie street life way of living was tied to throwing off the shackles of repressive Victorian sexual hypocrisy. Today, when everyone has a friend who is dying of AIDS, and three of four women you know have been sexually molested as a child (not to mention one out of every three men), and entire middle-class communities of Toronto suburban women are fearful of going onto their Etobicoke streets either in daylight or by night for fear of being raped, the very idea of a hedonistic free-style sexual abandonment seems so utterly irresponsible as to leave the bitter taste of bile on the tongue. But in 1965 it was different.

In Yorkville, in 1965, at the crash pads and in the coffeehouses and on the streets, everybody was nineteen and beautiful, or thought they were, or wished they were. And everyone who was nineteen and beautiful or thought they were or wished they were, everyone who had grown up in Orillia or Port Hope or Sturgeon Falls or South Mountain or North Gower, wanted to display their nineteenness and their beauty at the corner of Yorkville Street and Avenue Road, in the head shops on Yonge Street, and on the dimlit foredeck of the Riverboat.

Everybody was making love. Or at least they made what passed for love in 1965 in Yorkville.

And everyone was passing through. Everyone was in town just for a moment, on their way to Vancouver or to San Francisco or to Paris or to Marrakech. Everyone was coming from somewhere or going to someplace. There was a bohemian romance in the air.

Lightfoot was a big hit at the Riverboat. The royalty cheques were flowing in. Everybody wanted to be his friend, his collaborator, his lover. Nobody could pretend now that they had never heard of this Lightfoot guy before. Maybe he wasn't nineteen anymore, but so what? He couldn't have handled this gig at nineteen. There are always enough people around who are nineteen or who think they are or wish they were. Lightfoot could play the role of the veteran, the guy who's been everywhere, seen everything, met everyone.

But it's the suddenness that does them in. Whether they are rock-n-roll singers, or comedians or folksingers, there they are: yesterday they were struggling to make a hundred bucks a week playing the dingiest of bars and clubs in the boondocks, in places they've never even heard of until they got a gig there, and suddenly they're rich, able to afford the best food and wine of impeccable vintage, the best, softest, silk pillows and the finest home on the block and the best lovers money can buy.

So, people start saying they're weird. Ask anybody about Lightfoot, or Elvis, or McCartney, or Waylon, they'll tell you the same thing: what a weird guy.

The truth is, they're not weird at all. It's just that they start wondering: what do these people want? Yesterday, they were scrounging a few beers over at the tavern, trying to chat up the two young things over in the corner, trying to convince some cheap club owner to pay a few bucks for a whole evening of song and dance. Today, everybody wants to buy the drinks and share their dope, the young things pass their names and phone numbers written on the inside of Players cigarette packages, club owners are lining up to hand over a thousand bucks every week, and all the freebies thrown in besides. Why?

Why, indeed? Was Lightfoot any handsomer in 1965 than he had been in 1964? Was the newest song he had just written any better than the one he had written in 1963? Was his voice any more melodic than it had been in 1961? It's the suddenness that does you in.

It's normal. His friends noticed that Lightfoot was starting to change. He was becoming more closed in, more suspicious, more paranoid. Trusting no one, he began to withdraw into himself, a withdrawal which eventually became so complete that, in the end, nobody could claim that they really knew who this guy Gordon Lightfoot was.

In the music world, there's a rule of thumb about the suddenness. Grab whatever's offered as fast as you can, because you may never get another chance; only the very luckiest ever get a chance at what is euphemistically called a comeback, but what really is only an equally sudden halt to the steep nosedive a career can take after that amazing leap to the top of the hill. Only the very foolish believe that there is such a thing in show business as over-exposure. Colonel Tom Parker, Elvis Presley's manager, never worried about over-exposure. Brian Epstein, the Beatles' manager, never worried about over-exposure. Nor did Albert Grossman. It was under-exposure that could kill you.

So, Grossman had Lightfoot playing everywhere and being on every television show and being written about by every writer, until it seemed impossible that one person could be in so many places at once. He got Lightfoot that priceless green card so he could play the States. He got him on the *Tonight Show* with Johnny Carson.

Through Grossman, Lightfoot met Bob Dylan while he was in the States. They got along pretty well, although Lightfoot made the mistake of pretending he knew how to play pool and then got horribly beaten. He quickly learned the game and became as good as anybody who didn't earn his living hustling suckers in all the pool halls of all the cities of North America.

A decade later, Lightfoot ruefully admitted that he had met Dylan too early in his own career and that he had been nervous and over-awed meeting the person whose songs he had been singing for several years. In future years the two would be on a more equal footing, although no one has ever accused Dylan of treating other performers as equals: his normal attitude is usually one either of disdain or indifference. Such an attitude makes it difficult to carry on a conversation with him at the best of times, and it is no wonder that Lightfoot's nervousness would make their first few meetings social disasters.

Lightfoot hit the road and played the gigs and did the interviews. A thousand other folksingers would get this far in their careers and find their way blocked to anywhere else, either through lack of any real talent beyond the demands of the coffeehouse circuit, or through their devotion to the bottle, or through their love of the sweet cold needle in their veins. Not Lightfoot. He knew all of this was a game, and he was determined to play it as well as anyone. His new friend, Bob Dylan, wanted to be bigger than Elvis, bigger than the Beatles, bigger than anyone. Lightfoot never mentioned it out loud, but so did he.

All the gigging and all the touring and all the boozing and all the womanizing had broken up show business marriages before and probably will until the end of time. Lightfoot and Brita's marriage had little chance to be the exception. In fact, all those weeks and months on the road took the form of a sort of trial separation. Like many other marriages, the separations and reconciliations would continue for a while, but, in the meantime, the trials became more and more like the real thing, until the two became indistinguishable.

Lightfoot was, in fact, enjoying the freedom his new fame was bringing him. His first responsibility was to his career. Nobody else he met ever took the concept of fidelity seriously. Why should he? It was 1965, not 1865.

Who could take such infidelities from their husband and

With Fiedler at the Riverboat.

Bob Dylan in Toronto, 1964.

not scream and yell and cry about it? The arguments became more and more fierce. Now that there was a little more money, the boozing didn't really affect the family budget but it did bring out a surly, sarcastic, brutally coarse side of Lightfoot that only the most subservient, brutalized wife would ever stand for. And no one has ever described Brita in those terms.

Lightfoot did what husbands from time immemorial have done. He slipped out of town to work on the road.

Leaving Brita and little Fred in the basement apartment, Lightfoot fled to Detroit. There he crashed at Joni and Chuck Mitchell's walk-up apartment near Wayne University. If they were surprised to see him, they didn't let on, and welcomed him with the customary openheartedness that was typical of that group of mid-sixties people who were used to crashing at other people's places and habitually opened their doors to other crashers.

The Mitchells and Lightfoot had become friends while meeting on the coffeehouse circuit. Each had been impressed with the other's talent. The Mitchells, a fairly unconventional husband-and-wife team, had begun using Lightfoot material in their act. Lightfoot never returned the favour, although he did once admit that Joni's composition "Both Sides Now" was his favourite song. By this time, Lightfoot had reduced other people's material in his own act until it was barely one percent of all the compositions he sang. He was turning supply-and-demand into a one way street, allowing other people to use his material, but very seldom using any of theirs.

The Mitchells had chosen Detroit as their home base on the basis of some very interesting reasoning. First, there was Wayne University, which supplied a ready audience of students hungry for the sound of the new folk music. Detroit was accessible to all the American markets and yet it was close to the Canadian border, just across from Windsor.

*Joni and Chuck Mitchell in their walk-up apart-
ment in Detroit, 1966.* (Photo by Edwin
Lombardo, courtesy of the Detroit *News*)

Since Chuck was an American, his wife could work in the U.S. And since Joni was Canadian, her husband could travel freely into Canada. Green cards were a non-issue with the Mitchells (and, even today, that ubiquitous green card is still the most highly prized commodity a Canadian performer who wishes to work in the States can aspire to). And, there was radio station CKLW-Windsor.

CKLW is a twenty-four-hour broadcasting advertisement for the merits of free trade. Why? Because it is the biggest, the noisiest, the richest radio station in the Detroit market. And it's not even in Detroit, not even in the States, it's across the border in Windsor, Ontario. Well, everyone admits things are not exactly the same in the eighties as in the sixties, but it's still hot stuff. On another level, it's exactly the way it was in the sixties, for CKLW has now changed music formats and has become a "Music of Your Life" station, playing the music of nostalgia, playing the soft hits from twenty and thirty years ago, playing even the same Lightfoot records that they played two decades ago. In the sixties it was the best there ever was at doing what it did best.

CKLW was probably the best station in the whole wide world at breaking new hits. For decades, its staff was on the edge of sniffing out every new craze, every new sound that its admittedly American audience would go crazy for and spend millions of dollars to hear. Like many outsiders before and since, CKLW knew what Americans wanted better than the Americans themselves did.

And, for a while, CKLW knew that Americans wanted folk music. That perception played right into the hands of Joni and Chuck Mitchell, who were just across the river ready to give those Americans what they wanted most.

But American pop music consumers are, if nothing else, fickle and demanding. So, if Joni and Chuck were thinking that this folk music craze would, fuelled by the Top Forty list from CKLW, go on forever, the radio station was going to prove them wrong.

To be sure, at this time folk (and folk-rock, which was the upcoming style combining the beat of rock with the lyricism of folk), was really only a small part of the market. The Beatles and the Rolling Stones and the Animals and the Kinks and a hundred other pimply, whey-faced young boys from Britain were what was really happening in pop music. That was where the big money was. And, yet, don't forget that the North American market for anything, including pop music, is made up of 250 million people—a lot of people with different tastes, even if that taste is shamefully manipulated every day in a thousand different ways. So, while folk music may not have been exactly in the same league as the so-called British Invasion, there was still a huge and healthy market out there. Especially if radio stations like CKLW would get going and help promote it.

Unfortunately for all the folkies, CKLW decided (and correctly, too) that the next big thing, at least in the Detroit area, would be not folk music, but Motown music, roaring out of—of all places—Detroit itself. It was the music of Little Stevie Wonder and Smokey Robinson and the Miracles and Diana Ross and the Supremes, from the new independent company called Motown Records, headed by a young black entrepreneur called Berry Gordy. It was a natural for CKLW to promote this new music day and night. So much for the folk music boom in Detroit.

Folk music, like the British explosion happening at the same time, was primarily a music by and for white people. Except for the blues part of it, the Mississippi Delta guitar and vocal stylings imitated by a thousand young white guys who had never been near Mississippi in their lives, and wouldn't want to be found dead (not a totally remote possibility) near there, and apart from a handful of folk stylists like Odetta and Richie Havens and Harry Belafonte, American blacks ignored the folk music style. This was a kiss of death; for wherever black music goes, white music is right behind, adapting, borrowing and, ultimately, stealing.

In the summer of 1965, none of this mattered to Joni and
Chuck Mitchell and Gordon Lightfoot. They were doing all
right. Lightfoot was doing even a little better than that. But
for the moment, he was laying low in the Mitchells'
apartment, venturing forth to play a few gigs in the
Detroit-Windsor area, getting—as it was described in those
days—his head together, planning his next strategy, trying
to figure out if the next move within his marriage should be
towards reconciliation or divorce.

But the rest of the world wasn't standing still, and he
couldn't either. He had to grab those once-in-a-lifetime
opportunities.

He went back to Toronto.

By the summer of 1965, after years of being shunted
from venue to venue, the Mariposa Folk Festival seemed to
have found a permanent home in the resort area of
Caledon East, on Innis Lake, far from angry townsfolk and
meddling politicians. Heavy rains marred the festival for
most spectators, however, and Ian and Sylvia's opening
night concert had to be cancelled because of a power failure.

Lightfoot was once again invited to appear and he was a
hit with the fans, who were now beginning to know who he
was. Lightfoot was considered by the critics to have been the
best-received of the Canadian performers (as the years
went by, the cherished notion of an all-Canadian festival
had been quietly dropped), although a music critic review-
ing the festival sneered that it consisted of "elevated
rock-n-roll, bad poetry and shallow politics. But the audience seemed to love it."

Back in Toronto, Lightfoot made a new friend who
would share his music and partying for the next decade,
occasionally writing an article offering wry comments about
the life and times of his friend Lightfoot. Robert Markle,
visual artist, and Gordon Lightfoot, folksinger, became
unlikely buddies.

A more incongruous and ill-matched couple of friends would be hard to imagine: Lightfoot lean, lithe, well-groomed, a performer already aware of his image and his responsibility to adjust, correct and improve it for his public, in ways both large and small; and Markle, the overweight, bespectacled visual artist unconcerned about his physical appearance to the point where the description "slovenly" becomes almost a compliment.

Lightfoot's knowledge of the visual arts extended only as far as it affected him—in publicity photographs, in designs for posters and press releases and drawings for album covers. Markle listened to popular music only when he had to, considering it inherently inferior to jazz and classical music. "Bob Dylan and Mozart don't address the same artistic problems. Dylan doesn't even know what the problems are," he sneers.

But friends they became, a friendship stretching over two decades and, even if dormant, unto today. That they should meet at all was only coincidence.

Markle had come from his native Hamilton with a scholarship to study at the Ontario College of Art. Like most Canadian youngsters of his generation, his concept of art embodied only illustration and commercial art. But at the OCA, new worlds were opened to art students—the world of Gauguin and Picasso and Modigliani, the world of de Kooning, Pollock and Borduas, the world of New York, Paris and, perhaps, even Toronto when, in the near future, that good and clean city would take its place as one of the art capitals of the world. Markle was a keen student and his original interest in illustration was shaped into an abiding passion for the fine arts.

Markle had left the OCA and found a small studio in the heart of Toronto's downtown where he lived with his wife Marlene and painted, trying to find a style, a career and a reputation. By the fall of 1965, he had already had exhibitions at the Isaacs Gallery in Toronto, the Art Gallery of Ontario, the London Art Gallery, the Montreal Museum of Fine Arts and the Banfer Gallery in New York City. Markle was considered to be an up-and-coming young artist among the best of his generation in Canada.

Not all of his fellow students at the OCA had followed his example. Ken Rodmell, an old buddy from the art school, had become an art director on the *Canadian* magazine, a weekly insert in daily newspapers across the country featuring articles on sports, politics and entertainment of national interest.

The magazine was doing a story on the burgeoning folk music scene in town and Lightfoot was going to be featured. He was wearing a cool smile on his face. To be featured in the *Canadian* meant you had arrived. It was a wonderful publicity break. He was being taken seriously by the national media. Marshall McLuhan, the University of Toronto's communications philosopher, had not yet made the term "media" familiar to the world, but the media existed, and they could make or break a young career with approval or indifference.

Given the task of illustrating the upcoming article, Rodmell thought of his old art school buddy, Markle. He picked up the phone. Markle was interested. Ready cash was as hard to come by for a struggling artist in those days as it is today.

It was 1965 and Markle had never heard of Gordon Lightfoot.

A few days later, Lightfoot phoned Markle. After some polite chitchat, Markle suggested they meet the next day in his studio. "Bring along your guitar. And a bottle of Chivas Regal."

The next day, Markle was sitting with friends over a few draft beer at the Pilot tavern. The Pilot, at the corner of Bloor and Yonge, was a popular drinking spot for artists,

Lightfoot at a concert at Lakehead University in the early sixties.

intellectuals and students. It reputedly made the best burgers in town. Nobody minded if you nursed a beer for hours while reading or if noisy arguments developed over the finer points of existentialist philosophy or the merits of West Coast jazz over be-bop.

The Pilot had been described by sculptor Harold Town as "the world's oldest, floating avant-garde in the history of art," and in the tavern's back room on any given day could be found the artists who were trying to take over the city, the country and, ultimately, the world with their art: people like Markle and Graham Coughtry and Dennis Burton and Michael Snow and Michael Sarrazin and Donald Sutherland.

Markle drank up and bid farewell, mentioning he had to leave because he was meeting this folksinger Gordon Lightfoot in his studio for a portrait sitting.

Lightfoot knocked on the apartment door. Markle invited him in, apologizing for the smallness of the studio. For Lightfoot, still living with his wife and newborn in the small basement apartment a few streets away, its size seemed palatial. There followed the polite feeling-out of two professionals in different fields coming together on a collaboration.

Someone was at the door. Markle opened it to a couple of friends from the Pilot. He invited them in and turned back to Lightfoot.

They shared a jolt of the Chivas.

Lightfoot sat on a stool, strumming idly. Markle sat at his easel, giving instructions.

"Pretend you're giving a concert. I'll make a bunch of drawings. Don't worry when I throw paper on the floor. It's just the way I work. I'll make a hundred different impressions until I get something just right." Lightfoot seemed pleased to be a model.

Somebody else was at the door. Lightfoot sang a bit,

throwing his head back in his distinctive style. Markle drew a bit, heaping paper onto the floor.

Again, there was a knock on the door. The studio was getting crowded. Even if Markle didn't know who this Lightfoot guy was, everyone else at the Pilot did. And they all wanted to meet him.

Soon the small studio was jam-packed. Lightfoot didn't have to pretend he was in a club; the audience was right there, cheering wildly after every song, requesting songs that, in an incredibly short time, had already become favourites. Markle sketched madly, throwing unfinished attempts onto the studio floor, looking for the right expression, the perfect pose, the visual equivalent to what he was hearing.

If the experience was ego-building to Lightfoot, it was problematic to Markle. After all, he was supposed to be on the cutting edge of the young avant-garde. He should know about phenomena like this. He drew feverishly. He was onto something here. Lightfoot sang and joked and mumbled and strummed. The Chivas went down smoothly.

The friendship began.

Both Markle and Lightfoot were married. But, since their relationship had begun because of a professional association, they were able to continue as a twosome, excluding the women. This suited both, for different reasons. In the pop music world, women didn't really count. They were lovers, helpmates perhaps, wives even, people to return to after the gig, after the tour, after the recording session. They didn't really figure in the big scheme of things. In the visual arts world, there was more of a sense of sexual equivalence, often a more-or-less serious attempt to break down existing codes of sexual conduct, an acceptance of new ideas and philosophies about women's rights. But when it came to the work—the new painting, the new sculpture, the new film—if it was the male who was the artist, every new philosophy went out the window. Every aspect of life was subordinated to the creation of art. Simone de Beauvoir was a writer to be discussed late at night at the Pilot or the Purple Onion or the Brunswick House. Her ideas about women were not to intrude on daily living.

The friendship between the two men was based on four things: the size of Markle's apartment studio, booze, conversation and the search for women.

Since Lightfoot's basement apartment was so small, he began using Markle's place as a rehearsal hall. Markle liked having Lightfoot around, even if he sometimes found it unfair that Lightfoot seemed to create new songs so effortlessly, while he went through metaphysical hell creating a new painting.

One time, while they were playing pool, Markle baited Lightfoot about the slackness of his working habits.

"Why aren't you humming?" he asked, as Lightfoot set up a shot to the corner pocket.

"I don't see you drawing," replied Lightfoot, without looking up.

Markle's work was conducted by daylight. Lightfoot's was done under a spotlight in the darkness. In the between-hours, there was lots of time for the buddies to go pub-crawling. Despite its reputation as Toronto the Good, there was ample opportunity in the city for serious drinkers to quench their thirst. A draft beer cost fifteen cents. A bottle of beer was sixty-five cents. If you had fifty bucks in your pocket, you were rich.

Over drinks, they talked. And talked. And talked. There is no doubt that Markle was the more voluble of the two. He had an unquenchable thirst for new knowledge and an opinion on every possible topic. Lightfoot listened a lot but he too had opinions on most subjects, even if he found it easier to express himself in song and verse than in conversation.

Like many fundamentally shy people, Lightfoot always seemed reluctant to express himself even if what he did end up saying made ultimate sense. For the demands of his career, however, he was forced to speak in public, to be interviewed, to host television programs, to keep the pace of a concert interesting by between-songs monologue (indeed, folksingers were expected to illustrate their songs with anecdote and history, explaining who had written the song, where the singer had first heard it, and what the song meant to the singer and, one hoped, would mean to the audience). But for Lightfoot it has always been a struggle to overcome his basic shyness; sometimes it is even painful for the audience to watch him attempt to explain himself. Just as he had been back in Orillia, Lightfoot was most comfortable and self-confident (some have even called it self-important) when he was just playing his music and singing his songs.

His shyness didn't prevent him from pursuing personal success with vicious determination, however. Now that he was a star on the coffeehouse circuit, he was determined to leap even higher into the firmament.

Chapter 4

Rich Man's Spiritual

Lightfoot's meticulous and time-consuming attention to the demands of his career was already starting to break up his marriage; ultimately the career would win the struggle of fame and fortune against home and family. For a pop star, the demands of the road and the temptations of the road are loved and hated in equal measure. The road is a metaphor for all the struggles of the musician's soul.

The road is endless. When you are on the bottom, the road is a series of squalid bars in places nobody has ever heard of except for the people who live there; the road is the back seat of a huge, American-built sedan where you're squeezed between the drum set and the bass guitar, or the back of a van where you're lying on the floor, jolted by each bump of the unpaved road leading to the place the road map says you should have passed half an hour ago; the road is the bikers who attack each other with pool cues over some imagined slight not even understood by the other patrons cowering under formica tables clutching their glasses of draft beer; the road is a series of women who, enchanted somehow by the look and sound of a pop musician, whether that musician be a rock-n-roller, a country singer or a folkie, wait until the last waltz has faded away, wait until the equipment has been loaded into the sedan or the van, wait until the last remnants of chop suey in the all-night Chinese diner have been greedily consumed, and, having waited even until the first streaks of dawn are showing themselves in the east, ask for no more than that the musician who so enchants them treat them with shabbiness, with disrespect and, ultimately, with hatred. When you are on the bottom you know that the road is ugly and confidence-destroying. And you know that when you are on the top the road will be different.

The trouble is, when you do get to the top, the road is different but no less destroying. The sedan and the van have been replaced by the airplane and the limousine, the Chinese diner has been replaced by room service and the private back rooms of fancy French restaurants, the women are dressed better and are more sophisticated, less eager to wait for you, but there's less waiting, in any case, because roadies now load up the equipment and dismantle the sound and light system. In the end, however, it's all the same road; it's the same road taking you away from your wife and child, the same road driving you crazy with insomnia, the same road leading you into new demands and into new temptations. Lightfoot himself has recently admitted, "All these years, I've been confronted with female temptation. It makes bad husbands out of musicians."

Many performers love the road. They love the fact that they have no family responsibilities, no lawn to mow, no walls to be re-painted, no crying babies to remind them that there is life somewhere else than on the stage, in the hotel room and in the airplane taking them further on up the road.

Lightfoot began life on the road in earnest.

Fiedler was picking up the options in his contract, so Lightfoot had several gigs lined up at the Riverboat, as well as at other clubs across Canada and in the United States.

Club owners were digging into their pockets to come up with his asking price, and as his reputation grew during the fall of 1965, so did his audience.

In November, he was off on an American mini-tour, playing the Chess Mate in Detroit and Gerde's Folk City in New York, billed with Jim Kweskin and Paul Butterfield. As his home life worsened, he now made Detroit a second home, sometimes staying with the Mitchells and other times finding his own accommodation.

Introduced by Peter, Paul and Mary, he made an appearance at the 1965 Newport Folk Festival. The festival that year became a watershed in the short history of the sixties folk revival. It was that year that Bob Dylan, looking like "a fierce Spanish outlaw," and backed up by a group of musicians so sure of themselves that they called themselves simply The Band, introduced all the elements of rock music—steady 4/4 beat on pounding drums, throbbing electric bass, piercing electric guitar and growling Hammond B-3 organ—into what had been a sweetly simple home-grown music.

The Band had for a long time been regulars on the bar circuit of Ontario and New York State, backing up Ronnie Hawkins in a thousand different dives, then setting up on their own and touring as Levon and the Hawks and, finally, simply as The Hawks. Along the way, in a bar in Hamilton, Ontario, they had found a devoted fan in a girl named Cathy Smith, who was madly in love with the bandleader, Levon Helm, and who would soon enter into Gordon Lightfoot's world.

The Band had recently moved to Woodstock, New York, where they worked on their own music and rehearsed with Bob Dylan, who had decided to shed his folkie image and front a rock band. The music they would create was going to change the folk revival movement overnight.

In the summer of 1965, at the Newport Folk Festival,

Dylan and The Band unveiled to the public the music they had been rehearsing up in Woodstock.

The audience was enraged. They booed. Dylan, the spiritual and musical leader of the folk movement, was hissed and booed and forced off the stage by his most devoted fans, the devotees of his Woody Guthrie-like hobo-bohemian music. Newport went berserk.

Folk purists like Pete Seeger, who had almost singlehandedly kept the spirit and truth of folk music alive since its last revival in American in 1949, were saddened. Fellow folk revivalists of the sixties, like Phil Ochs and Joan Baez, reviled Dylan for his betrayal of all the ideals by which they lived.

After his electric set, Dylan went offstage, the boos and hisses ringing in his ears. It is said that Pete Seeger was so dismayed by the new music that he was crying. Dylan went back onstage to mollify the crowd with an acoustic version of one of his new songs, "It's All Over Now, Baby Blue."

Dylan was hurt by the rejection. But he was right and he knew he was right. All the rest of them could wallow in self-righteousness and self-defined musical purity, but he wanted to evolve and redefine the meaning of the folk movement. Dylan was the first to realize that it was not the bohemian artsiness of musicians looking backwards into an ill-defined, hazy musical heritage which was America's real folk music, but the raw, shrill voices of urban rock-n-roll which truly sang from the people. In one afternoon at the Newport Folk Festival, Dylan put a loud, arrogant and early end to the acoustic folk revival movement which, after all, was only a few years old in 1965. Nobody noticed it at the time. Except, perhaps, for Dylan himself.

Certainly not Gordon Lightfoot. He appeared before Dylan's famous electric set, along with Peter, Paul and Mary, singing several cuts from his soon-to-be-released album. He left the folk trio the honour of singing his song, "For Lovin' Me." After all, it was they who had the hit record of the song. Most of the American audience were hearing and seeing Lightfoot for the first time. Peter, Paul and Mary were already stars.

The audience liked Lightfoot. He was their kind of folk. It can be seen as wry irony that he was far better received than the new Dylan. For Lightfoot did not disappoint the crowd; he did not add thundering drums and booming bass and screeching guitar to his songs; he sang the sweet melodies of his songs with no accompaniment, and the audience appreciated him for it.

The battle lines between the acoustic purists and the electric rebels had been harshly drawn and Lightfoot had remained with the conservative forces. Over the next few years, he would make small concessions to the rebels, partly because he never lost his admiration for Dylan and partly because commercial considerations demanded electrification to some degree.

On Dylan's part, he would vent his hurt and his anger in his next single, titled "Positively Fourth Street," in which he castigated his former fans and members of the folkie community with all the rage and venom he could muster in three minutes and fifty-three seconds.

Perhaps it is because Lightfoot did not follow Dylan's lead and immediately form a rock band that his career has lasted as long as it has. Perhaps if all the other folkies—McGuinn and Crosby of the Byrds and Phillips and Doherty of the Mamas and the Papas and Simon and Garfunkel and Judy Collins and Joni Mitchell and Yanofsky and Sebastian of the Lovin' Spoonful and Tom Rush and, eventually, even Phil Ochs and Joan Baez—perhaps if all of them embraced Dylan's new music which they soon called, in an attempt to preserve some integrity and history, "folk-rock," there was the need for one person to resist change and to become a familiar voice which would retain all its original virtues while musical chaos ruled elsewhere.

To be sure, having spent years arriving at an authentic voice and style for himself, Lightfoot was not about to throw it away on a path that might lead only to failure and obscurity. Dylan had the talent and the intelligence to make his new music work for himself but he was the only person who knew exactly what he was doing and, after Newport 1965, even Dylan became dismayed at the number of folkies who traded their Martin acoustic guitars for Fender electric ones. After all, hadn't he advised everybody in song not to follow leaders?

Perhaps realizing intuitively that no one could possibly beat Dylan at his own game—and, God knows, a thousand other musicians tried and failed—Lightfoot quite correctly perceived that he now had the possibility of becoming the biggest star in the much smaller field of the remaining acoustic folksingers. In the long run, if the musicologists and critics attacked him for what they perceived as a safeness and a sameness, he might nevertheless make many more fans and, equally importantly, much more money than his critics ever dreamed possible. Like Dylan, he knew what he was doing and all the booing and carping would not deter him. He would stay with his own style and see where it led him.

During that magic year of 1965, as everything seemed to just fall in place for Lightfoot, his energy level was pushed to maximum and, despite his public image as a laid-back, folksy, hesitant sort of guy, he was racing through a schedule, both in his private and professional lives, that would destroy most normal people. And, unlike almost everybody else in the music business, he was not living to the rhythm of uppers and downers, he was living so high on success that he needed only one downer to keep him on even keel, the downer of Chivas Regal and Johnny Walker and dry red wine.

He was racing through his life, hardly pausing to enjoy

any of it. But there were so many places to go, so many commitments to keep. His first single came out in mid-summer. "I'm Not Sayin'" hit the charts and, while not exactly a million-seller, made his voice familiar to millions of radio listeners and added another reason for him to demand a high price for each appearance in public.

He toured to any folk club, legion hall or school gymnasium that would book him. Another American country singer, George Hamilton IV, recorded a Lightfoot composition, "Steel Rail Blues." Lightfoot played rhythm guitar on the cut. While in the U.S., he recorded Dylan's song "Just Like Tom Thumb's Blues," giving it a gentle, wistful interpretation that was, perhaps, far from what Dylan had in mind when he wrote it, but an interpretation that could stand as definitive save for Dylan's own. It was released as Lightfoot's second single, a reminder to the rest of the folk world that, while Lightfoot wasn't going to follow Dylan into the savagery of folk-rock, he was aware of exactly what was going on and that he could twist things around to suit his own ultimate purpose.

And, finally, he started getting the awards and prizes that signify emergence as the best of the class. In 1965, Lightfoot won the Gold Leaf Award as Folksinger of the Year. The Gold Leaf Awards were given by *RPM Magazine* through readership poll and were the forerunners to the Juno Awards, which were created later when the Canadian recording industry was more powerful and more sure of itself. To be named Folksinger of the Year meant beating out such competition as Ian and Sylvia, Joni Mitchell, Leonard Cohen and Bruce Cockburn. It was sweet repayment for all the energy expended during the year. And, completing a tricky double play, he also won an award from the music publishing association ASCAP for the best country song of the year, for "Ribbon of Darkness," recorded by Marty Robbins.

At the end of 1965, if Lightfoot had looked back on the events of the year, even he would have been amazed at the changes wrought by time and circumstance. A year earlier he had been struggling to make a hundred bucks a week when work was available. A year earlier there were only a few hundred people who knew who he was. A year earlier, he was a one man band, trying to singlehandedly figure out where he fit into the scheme of the music business.

All of a sudden he was becoming a rich man. His friend Markle noticed that, at first, Lightfoot wasn't aware of how rich he was becoming. He had the Grossman organization to figure these things out for him. Unlike John Phillips of the folk-rock group the Mamas and the Papas, Lightfoot never forgot twenty-five-thousand-dollar cheques in the glove compartment of his car but it nevertheless took him a while to comprehend the financial change that had occurred in so short a time. From a hundred dollars a week, he had in one year made several hundreds of thousands of dollars. And, from the knowing few who had followed him from folk club to folk club only a short while earlier, he was now a well-known star who could pack halls in two countries.

But things weren't perfect yet.

It had been a whole year since Lightfoot had recorded his album for United Artists, and it still hadn't been released. Lightfoot had spent long hours worrying about their hesitation. A career can be blown to smithereens by the mistiming of an album release. Lightfoot was lucky that, unlike many rock acts, his style and material did not significantly change in one year but he had had to scramble and make do with singles when he knew perfectly well that his audience bought albums and were not the sort of people who followed the Hit Parade or the Top Forty or the Top Ten singles hits. He wanted his album Lightfoot released, and soon.

United Artists had spent most of the year dithering over the merits of the album they had bought from Grossman. On the one hand, it sounded pleasant and professional enough, but they didn't think it contained the obvious single that would zoom to the top of the charts and carry the album behind. Unlike some other record companies (Elektra and Columbia, for example), United Artists was a singles-oriented company and was hesitant when faced with an album that didn't seem to have any singles potential at all. For all the critical acclaim, albums by Dylan, Baez and Peter, Paul and Mary on other labels didn't send the cash registers into a ringing frenzy.

On top of that, after the 1965 Newport Festival and the release of Dylan's first really electrified single, "Like a Rolling Stone," which did sell a million records and make the Top Ten, the people at United Artists weren't sure anymore that an acoustic album could even repay its costs.

Still, nobody at the record company could argue with the fact that Lightfoot was getting bigger and bigger every day and, even without the album, was gaining a devoted following in the hinterlands of Canada and the States and, furthermore, that lots of other people were getting hits out of his songs. So, finally, after failing to meet several other projected release dates, United Artists promised that the album would come out in the New Year. If it didn't sell, they could always claim that the album was a prestige release meant to showcase a new talent rather than make a lot of money.

Lightfoot was relieved. The album release would fit into his plans for 1966. His fledgling career might have come to an abrupt and early end if UA had decided not to release the album at all.

Then there was his personal life. Lightfoot had managed to spend the last six months of 1965 away from home, away from the bickering and the fighting and the arguments. He was happiest on the road, where nobody dared confront him with responsibility, where everyone applauded him and told him how wonderful he was, where he could lose himself in the lyrics and the melodies of his newest songs, where everybody bought him one more drink and passed him one more toke, where the pretty girls took him to their beds and, sometimes, to their hearts, and where each town disappeared on the road behind him when the gig was over, so that he could become the drifting wanderer of his own songs.

His life with Brita was becoming an existence of reliable pattern, with separation and reconciliation repeated a hundred times until it became the only possible method of survival. Brita was the first of several women who fit into this pattern. Each of the women who followed her were sure they were to be the one to change history. But, in his own way, Lightfoot was to be a constant lover.

On the last day of December 1965, Brita had given birth to their second child, a girl they called Ingrid. By this time, and Brita wasn't even aware of it, the marriage was already falling apart. A major reason for the failure was that each wanted something completely different in life. Brita, from the wrong side of the Stockholm tracks, was seeking a safe bourgeois existence, a life of stability based on family, home and money. Despite the love he once felt for Brita, Lightfoot wanted the opposite—an exciting bohemian existence. Lightfoot would never sneer at money, but the safeness and dullness of a middle-class family life held no attractions for him. Asked when he knew that his marriage to Brita was over, he now replies, "Before it even began."

Nobody, least of all Lightfoot, was worried about a way of life becoming repeatable and never-ending in the first days of January, 1966. The awards ceremonies were over, the hit singles were riding high on the charts, and there was the next engagement at the Riverboat to look forward to.

Ingrid and Fred Lightfoot.

Nobody, least of all Lightfoot, was aware that he was about
to meet the second great love of his life.

By this, his third engagement at the Riverboat, in the
dead of winter but the brightness of January, Fiedler no
longer had to worry about his thousand dollars. He only
wished he had a bigger club, so that he could hold ten times
as many people and make ten times as much money. By
now, he was almost pleased to turn over the cheque, pleased
as only a club owner can be when he knows the payment is a
sure-fire investment. Lightfoot was happy to be at the
Riverboat. It had become his home-town stand, where he
could bask in the adulation of a crowd who had not
discovered him only in the past few months, but had been
following him and his music for a long time. Fiedler was
happy to have Lightfoot at the Riverboat. Having taken the
chance on paying Lightfoot's price, he was pleased to have
been proven so perspicacious. The two became fast friends.
True to form in keeping all his friends separate from one
another, Lightfoot didn't introduce Markle to Fielder for
another half-decade.

That same month, the self-titled *Lightfoot* album was
released by United Artists. The reviews were solid, but for
some reason it didn't sell as well as either Lightfoot or
Grossman had thought it would. Self-doubt began creeping
in. Perhaps folk music really was dead. Perhaps it was only
that another triumph would be too much for a mere human
to accept gracefully and the gods had decreed that, for the
first time in a year, only a semi-triumph was to be permitted
to someone who had already triumphed so much more than
his fellows. Or else it was simply that United Artists, with all
its hesitations and ditherings, had waited far too long to
release the album and time had passed it by.

Even today, people still think that *Lightfoot* is his best
album. If all the people who claim to have grown up on that
album actually had bought it, then it really would have been

Dylan and members of The Band at Massey Hall, 1965.

a bestseller. It certainly is a showcase for the early-sixties style of contemporary folk music, before folk added rock to its repertoire. Today, it seems to personify, along with only half a dozen other folk albums, everything that was decent and gentle and idealistic about folk music, with no elements of the narcissism and amateurism and self-righteousness that were part of the folk scene now best forgotten.

There are critics who think that Elvis Presley never did anything as fine, as pure, as passionate as his first sessions with Sun Records in Memphis in 1954, which is not to say that they argue that everything he did after that was worthless. Perhaps Lightfoot's first album can be seen in the same context. Was it the recording into which he poured all the passion, all the craft, all the energy he had as a young man? Did he so drain himself musically that the rest of his long career can be seen as only footnotes to the achievement of his first record on United Artists?

The cover shows an impossibly-young Lightfoot seated upon a director's chair, holding his guitar high over his left shoulder, picking out a chord and looking into the emptiness on his right, his legs stretched out long in front of him and crossed at the ankles.

He looks like a James Dean sitting in that chair with his sleeves carelessly rolled up towards the elbows, his head averted and eyes searching for something—an unseen enemy, perhaps?—or as if he was about to answer an unseen questioner, about to answer the question, "Who is Gordon Lightfoot?"

Inside the album, the songs partially answer the question, even if they sometimes avoid confrontation with fear and loneliness and despair by singing softly about men who are trees and women who are birds nesting in their branches, and about men who take all the love a woman offers and leave town in the morning, and men who refuse to say that they love but they will try—all of these metaphors and similes used to confine relationships and feelings within the boundaries of a pop song.

A year had passed since he had recorded the album. He had logged a lot of psychic and geographical miles since then. Now, the millions of people in the record-buying public would finally be able to tell him whether his career would stumble and remain mired in the endless grind of one-night stands of increasing seediness or whether he might be bigger than Dylan, bigger than Elvis, bigger than the Beatles, even.

Or else, he might find his place somewhere in between.

Chapter 5

Airs and Rounds

His new album on the market and his January gig at the Riverboat breaking attendance records, Lightfoot's career was moving into high gear in the cold days and nights of January in 1966. Accompanied by John Stockfish on bass and Red Shea on guitar, he was hitting his first stride as a singer and connecting with the wildly enthusiastic audience at the Riverboat. It seemed that Toronto was adopting him as a Local Boy Who Made Good, showering him with adulation and affection.

During one of his appearances at the Boat, he met the woman who was to be the second great love of his life. Her name was Cathy Evelyn Smith. She was a waitress there. Cathy Smith, then eighteen, was part of that strange band of young women who are infatuated by musicians, follow them, wait for them until the first rays of dawn, make love to them, and hang around with them. Despite all the pretensions that she might make of her life, despite the hopes of her mother, despite the best efforts of the Ontario school system and the church of her childhood, Cathy Smith was—let's face it—a groupie.

This is not to say that groupies are necessarily sneered at, it is just that groupies fulfil for musicians the same purpose that sailors demand when they arrive screaming and yelling into port; and the women who stroll the waterfront of Halifax Harbour have a more serious attitude to the business at hand. Groupies tend to think in terms of romance and love, while constantly being humiliated and demeaned by the very musicians they so idolize.

Perhaps the most famous groupies of the sixties were the American duo known as the Plaster Casters, after their penchant for taking plaster-of-paris moulds of the sexual organs of their favourite rock stars (Mick Jagger was reputed to have been among the most favourably endowed, which did not at all hurt his reputation as a rock-n-roll lover). Jazz-rocker Frank Zappa penned an ode to an unknown groupie he called "Suzie Creamcheeze." Age seems not to be a factor in groupiedom: Hank Williams, Jr., lost his virginity at age fourteen to a woman who, if she could not make love with his father (who was dead), would be content to forever remind herself that she made it with his son; and one of the great scenes in the movie *Alice's Restaurant* is that of Arlo Guthrie escaping from the erotic designs of a woman who clearly had his father, Woody Guthrie, in mind when she made her move on Arlo. Perhaps the ultimate in the relationship between rock musicians and groupies occurred in the mid-sixties when it was revealed that Brian Jones, a member of the Rolling Stones until shortly before his death by drowning, had in one year made love to over four hundred women (Jones had kept a diary). This led one wag to comment that this pace did not allow Jones even the luxury of a one-night stand.

In any case, Cathy Smith was a groupie, even if not one whose voracious sexual appetite for musicians would classify her among the most renowned.

An orphan adopted by a family in Burlington, Ontario, Cathy had made her first ventures into the twilight world of musicians and female fans at the age of about fourteen, when she began accompanying a girlfriend to bars in nearby Hamilton to hear rock music. At lot of make-up and a little hair-styling went a long way to create the appearance of a twenty-one-year-old, especially when bartenders and bouncers were none too keen to throw out attractive young females, no matter what age.

Her favourite group quickly became Levon and the Hawks, a blues-oriented group consisting of four Canadians and an American (Levon of the band's name) who would, after they had changed their name to The Band, soon become one of the most important (some critics argue they became the most important) rock group of the 1960s. No one can really argue Cathy's ear for music; among the musicians she favoured with her presence were The Band, Lightfoot and the Rolling Stones.

At the age of seventeen, she had become pregnant by Levon, gave birth to a daughter she named Tracy Lee and moved to Toronto to support herself and her child. Bernie Fiedler gave her a job waitressing. Working at the Riverboat would be a perfect job for a sixties groupie, putting her in contact with the endless stream of musicians who passed through on the folk music circuit.

One night, after work at the Riverboat, Lightfoot and a friend went partying. They bumped into Cathy and Joyce Ivall, the girl who had originally introduced her to the bars of Hamilton. The four of them ended up in a two-bedroom apartment. Lightfoot and Smith ended up in one of the bedrooms.

They began seeing each other. When Lightfoot visited her in her rooming house, they would make love on the floor while baby Tracy slept on the bed.

Lightfoot confided his marital difficulties. Although he and Brita had recently moved to a spacious duplex on Farnham Avenue in the Yonge and St. Clair area, he explained that his marriage was in deep trouble and that his wife was staying with him only because she could see that he was now becoming a success and she wanted the economic benefits. He seemed convinced of the truth of this argument.

Whatever the state of his marriage, Lightfoot was not yet ready for a major affair; so, for the moment, he abandoned his young groupie. After the Riverboat gig, he was off on a major tour of Britain, as part of a folk package with Ian and Sylvia.

The folk music scene in Britain was completely different from the one in North America. For starters, Britain had a true oral folk tradition stretching back into prehistory; a folk tradition encompassing Elizabethan rounds, Morris dances, Celtic airs, and laments from the industrial revolution; a folk tradition kept alive by numerous clubs (such as the Workers' Music Association and the English Folk Song and Dance Society) often dedicated to preserving other aspects of English tradition, such as village greens and church fairs and real ale; a tradition, encouraged by academic research by Cecil Sharp, Ewan McColl and A.L. Lloyd, among others, and serious productions of BBC radio, such as "Ballads and Blues" and "Country Magazine." Folk music was a serious endeavour in Britain.

The collection and preservation of folk music there was tied to political correctness. The oral tradition in folk music was seen to be a part of the struggle towards the New Jerusalem, whereby the common folk expressed one part of the class struggle through the music they created in protest against the injustices imposed upon them by the ruling class. Eventually, in the sixties, the analysis of folk music became a battle among the Trotskyites, the Marxists and the Socialists of England—Conservatives (as usual bewildered by any notion that their purpose in life was actually to conserve anything) getting to the job at hand of destroying everything that had made Britain a great colonial power, building foreign-financed high-rises, reno-vating flats to rent at excessive rates and exporting London Bridge and the Queen E. ocean liners to add a few quid to the corporate treasury. The national balance-of-payments ledger was inked in black so long as John Lennon, Paul McCartney, George Harrison and Ringo Starr could con-tinue exporting records to America and as long as North Sea oil could be mortgaged to the future.

There was a subgenre of serious British folk music in the sixties, similar to North American contemporary folk. It included the singer Donovan, who surfaced from the Cock Club in St. Albans to have several international hits (including "Universal Soldier" and "Mellow Yellow"), and the certifiably insane Roy Harper who, unfortunately for this story, was once described by flautist Ian Anderson of the rock group Jethro Tull as "a great acoustic player who wipes the floor with all your James Taylors, Gordon Lightfoots, Dylans."

But, in general, British folk musicians in the sixties were restricted to the small clubs which catered to the fans of traditional folk music (that is, the songs handed down from generation to generation) and it would be some time yet until Bert Jansch, John Renbourn, Richard and Linda Thompson and Sandy Denny would finally emerge as the core musicians in a series of English groups which com-bined folk music and electric rock in some of the finest British music created in the seventies: Fairport Convention, Pentangle and Steeleye Span.

For the moment, none of this really mattered. Folk music, or folk-rock, or whatever you wished to call it, was only a tiny part of the music being consumed by an ever-growing population of young people eager to part with their dollars to connect with the electric sound which seemed to define their very beings.

There had been several explosions of popular consump-

tion of recorded music since the creation of the phonograph and the invention of the radio: in the forties, it was
the swing music of Benny Goodman and Artie Shaw and
Duke Ellington; in the mid-fifties it was the rock-n-roll of
Elvis and Little Richard and Chuck Berry; in the early
sixties it had been the "British Invasion" (a typically
arrogant American way of describing music which had the
effrontery of being produced by foreigners) of the Beatles
and the Rolling Stones and the Dave Clark Five. In the
mid-sixties, folk-rock was only a minor genre, easily outsold
by the beat of the Motown sound of a dozen black groups
and, already hearing the sound of the next wave of musical
innovation to capture the ears of America's record buyers,
the San Francisco sound or, as it was sometimes referred to,
"Acid Rock."

For the moment, the Lightfoots and the Dylans and the
Baezes had to compete, not only with their fellow folkies
who had seized electrification as the key to their success
with the record-buying public, but also with the Motown
sounds of the Supremes and the Four Tops and the
Marvelettes and the Temptations and, even further still,
with the continued success of the originators of the "British
Invasion," the four lads from Liverpool (John, Paul,
George and Ringo) who, you would think, would have
already exhausted whatever wellspring of inspiration they
had ever drawn from, but who seemed to continue to
re-create popular music with every visit to a recording
studio.

With their ever-continuing success in North America, the
Beatles were singlehandedly redeeming Britain's annual
balance-of-payments deficit, a wry commentary on the state
of British business affairs in general. Even the Royal Family
was forced to reckon with the Beatles' financial acumen and
success, first, by inviting them to attend a Command
Performance and, later, by bestowing upon each of them

the royal order of Commander of the British Empire. Other Commanders, who had earned their distinction by the honourable tradition of purchasing their command through charitable contributions, mounted a campaign of returning their medals in protest. In cynical turnabout, Beatle John Lennon, after he had left the group, eventually returned his medal to the Queen to protest that one of his records, "Cold Turkey," had not reached the Top Ten. As an afterthought, he also proposed that the return of his medal be considered as his disapproval of the war in Vietnam.

It is in this context that the British can be seen to have been ill-prepared for people like Lightfoot and Ian and Sylvia calling themselves folksingers, who seldom sang a song more than six months old and who unabashedly considered themselves to be part of the pop music scene, struggling to achieve the financial success of an Elvis Presley or a Paul McCartney. However, perhaps partly because every British citizen has a cousin in Toronto or a great-aunt in Victoria, the Canadian folksingers were popular and their tour was a mild success. The crowds were appreciative, if mildly uncomprehending, and the reviews were polite.

The tour completed, Lightfoot returned to Toronto to hurl himself into a schedule as hectic as the year before. He did not resume his affair with Cathy Smith.

His *Lightfoot* album was moving up in the folk music charts. George Hamilton IV's single of "Steel Rail Blues" became a bestselling country hit in both Canada and the United States. Country outlaw Waylon Jennings recorded his version of "For Lovin' Me." Lightfoot himself released a new single called "Spin, Spin." It quickly rose into the Canadian Top Ten. Nineteen sixty-six was becoming his best year yet. He eagerly grabbed every opportunity that came his way.

He became an occasional host on the CBC entertainment magazine television show *After Four*, interviewing and performing with many of his fellow folkies. He increased his touring schedule further, hitting the clubs and concert halls whenever he could get a booking. In June, he was once more jamming them in at the Riverboat and getting the best reviews of his young career. He made a widely-noted appearance on the TV show *Music Canada*, as part of that show's "Prelude to Expo 67." In August of 1966, he made his fourth appearance at the Mariposa Folk Festival, once again held on Innis Lake. He appeared with established folk performers Pete Seeger, Doc Watson, Ian Tyson and David Rea (who was stepping out on his own now, after accompanying Lightfoot on the first album and touring with Ian and Sylvia) and, newcomers to the festival scene, Joni Mitchell, the Stormy Clovers (Pete Hodgson and Susan Janes) and David Wiffen. Accompanied on guitar by the ever-present Red Shea and on bass by Paul Wiedman, Lightfoot gave a concert that both the crowd and the Toronto *Globe and Mail* agreed was "assured and composed."

A new critical complaint appeared in print for the first time, one voiced by the Toronto *Star*, which noticed that Lightfoot seemed "to be growing aloof from his audience."

The question of authenticity and being true to one's roots is one often raised by critics and academics who look at folk and pop music. Audience members and performers themselves seldom address the question except in the most oblique ways (as audience members, by forsaking performers who have seemingly gotten too upscale; as performers, by periodic returns to the source, real or imagined, of their original inspirations).

As a singer with a small-town background, Lightfoot had thus far been easily accepted by both audience and critics as an "unsophisticated" talent who, by virtue of his upbringing, was assumed to have had intimate contact with the rural virtues which are always seen as the strength of life in North America: love of the land, rugged honesty, self-effacement, the belief in Christian ethics and a sense of community. Film director John Ford, actor Jimmy Stewart and singer Hank Williams have, like Lightfoot, been assumed by fans and critics to embody these rural virtues in the work that they have created.

It is often difficult for these performers to fulfil the idealistic expectations of their critics, however. In considering Lightfoot, the factor which makes discussion of authenticity difficult is the same one that must be taken into consideration when discussing a blues singer like Muddy Waters, or a rock-n-roll singer like Elvis Presley, or a country singer like Waylon Jennings: at what point does a performer lose contact with the very meaning of his birthright?

Despite being considered by audience and critics as "one of the folk," any entertainer in a rural environment is never really like the other people in his community. Everyone else in Orillia, or in any other rural centre, works at the gas station or at the laundry or has a farm somewhere outside of town. The moment someone like Lightfoot raises his voice in song—for another person it might be writing a novel or building a sculpture—he immediately distances himself from the rest of "the folk," who have little hope of ever escaping from the minor rewards their toil might bring, even if they bring their skills into the city.

Lightfoot himself was set apart even as a child in Orillia, marked as a person who could someday escape the trivialization of his life by making something of himself in the outside world. Like his friends Croxall and Branch and Whelan, he was never considered, from the time he was a kid, to be one of "the folk."

Moreover, the rural virtues which a "folk" singer like Lightfoot is supposed to embody no longer exist in a world where television and computers and high school education conspire to level every life experience to a standard defined by the latest tools of demographic research. The Orillia that Lightfoot is expected to represent exists only in the imagination of Stephen Leacock.

Furthermore, when someone like Lightfoot moves from his rural childhood into his urban adulthood he enters the world of commerce and business. Everything about that world—making records, giving concerts, touring from town to town—is geared to business considerations; and the verities of rural life, idealized or not, no longer apply.

The "aloofness" that the *Star* reviewer noticed was not in his imagination. It existed, and was normal. It would be nice to think that a person like Lightfoot could carve a career for himself in the harsh world of the international music business without becoming alienated from the very audience he was trying to reach, but it is an unrealistic expectation. It took Elvis three years from the time he burst into the public consciousness before he withdrew into his shell of isolation; it took the Beatles about the same time; Lightfoot, after all, had already been a professional entertainer for a half-decade. Aloofness was to be one of his methods of survival. Woody Guthrie and Henry David Thoreau may have retained their links to the common folk by a studied cultivation of poverty and rootlessness, but this should not be expected from pop musicians. In this respect, Lightfoot was more akin to a Bob Dylan or a Pierre Trudeau than to a Guthrie or to a Thoreau.

For here is the hard kernel of truth: by 1966, Lightfoot was more of a Torontonian—more urbanized, more self-alienated, more isolated—than he was the rural oracle which his many fans believed him to be. The sadness of this truth lies in the fact that you really can take the country out of the boy. Nobody ever likes to admit it, that's all.

By virtue of being a Torontonian, he was now part of the national life of Canada.

His music was everywhere: on TV, on the radio, in concert, on the folk charts, on the country charts, on the pop charts. Clearly, he was as close to the top of the heap as a Canadian ever gets.

Finally, in September of 1966, the Grossman organization had to admit that in one short year Lightfoot had done something that they had considered impossible: he had become as over-exposed in the Toronto market as was healthy for his young career. Afraid that even his most loyal fans would one day grumpily admit that too much of a good thing is more than enough and turn their affections to some other performer, they drastically cut down Lightfoot's schedule, cancelling his *After Four* appearances, declining Toronto-area engagements and severely curtailing any future concerts at the Riverboat. This from a management company that really did not believe in the very idea of over-exposure.

If Lightfoot was not over-exposed in Canada, he was at least exposed as much as was really good for him. By the end of 1966, he had once again won the Best Country Song of the Year award, for "Steel Rail Blues," and "Spin, Spin" had just become Number One on the Canadian pop charts. He was easily outdistancing Canada's previous pop phenomenon, Ottawa's Paul Anka.

Lightfoot had clearly made the correct decision in keeping to his soft, folk-ballad approach to popular music. While the many new Yorkville singers and groups fumbled with decisions about whether to follow the pop trends of the black singers of Motown or to try to "Briticize" themselves with a Liverpool-cum-Toronto sound, Lightfoot continued his own acoustic way, following in the path already laid down by Dylan, Ian and Sylvia and Peter, Paul and Mary, taking the music to new dimensions even if all these people abandoned acoustic music for the newer sounds of rock music or electrified country music.

In Toronto, and in the rest of Canada and even across all of North America, a huge network of locally-owned clubs and coffeehouses was being created; a network which was providing a distribution system to Lightfoot's sort of music and the music of his fellows; a network not controlled by New York or Los Angeles or Nashville; a network which—in conjunction with the folk festivals which were springing up across the country—could consciously build up a Canadian audience for Canadian acts. It should have surprised no one that, in the seventies, when the network collapsed, the influx of new Canadian folk performers also died.

There is something uniquely Canadian in the fact that whenever a capitalist business appears, there appears alongside it a parallel phenomenon—that of a non-profit group offering the same service for free (most often paid for by taxpayers, whether they use the service or not). In the U.S., Republicans and libertarians would never stand for it but there is a unique quality to Canada which often allows the poorest and most misbegotten Canadian citizens access to services that would normally be considered (in a more capitalistic country) to be accessible only to the most wealthy. It is one of the most charming aspects of this country and one that is every day being sold away for the pittance of a trade concession or a favourable ruling concerning the sale of shakes or shingles or carburetors or premium crude oil.

Please do not expect Gordon Lightfoot to understand this Canadian phenomenon or to approve of it since he has made his untold millions without ever using any free distribution system which this country may have created (while some of the most celebrated of Canadian entertainers have made extensive use of the grants offered by the

In concert, 1965.

Canada Council); but alongside the commercial world of
the coffeehouses and clubs there grew up a parallel system
of folk clubs in the legion halls, YMCA's and church
basements of the country. These amateur clubs became
another way by which new folksingers and guitarists could
learn their craft.

In Toronto, perhaps the most famous was in the basement of the Bloor Street United Church, on Bloor near St.
George. It was called Fat Albert's. Lightfoot never played
Fat Albert's but a thousand young folksingers did in the
years after 1966, and every one of them knew the lyrics and
chords to "For Lovin' Me" and "Early Morning Rain."

Among the youngsters who first began picking guitars
and singing at Fat Albert's and at the Whistlestop, a Sunday
evening floating hootenanny held at different YMCAs
across Toronto, were Neil Young, Dan Hill, Mose Scarlett
and Raffi. One of the most eccentric of the young performers
was Leon Redbone who, from his earliest days, cultivated a
deliberate air of mystery. Nobody ever knew where Redbone lived. The only place he could be contacted was in the
pool hall in the Bloor subway station. When Redbone
emerged from the amateur clubs to pursue his recording
career in the seventies, he had lost none of his mystery.

The burgeoning amateur clubs were to provide to
Lightfoot, and to his fellow folkies on the professional
circuit, an ever-widening circle of young devotees of his
style of music, a circle of people who, once they got into the
habit of buying his records and attending his concerts,
would continue these habits into the middle age of their
adulthood.

In that same year of 1966, the year of national prepara-
tion for the upcoming World Exposition to be held in
Montreal in 1967, a wave of quickening nationalism swept
Canada—or perhaps it was two waves: one in English-
Canada and an even more emotional one in Quebec. For

the first time in its century-long history, and perhaps for the last, there was a feeling of well-being and pride in all things Canadian. Lightfoot's small-town Canadian style, his understated presentation, his frequent references in music to things all Canadians were familiar with, his whole approach to his audience, which seemed to be totally non-American and home-grown—all these combined to make him the embodiment of a national consciousness, a consciousness which reverberated with his audience. He was one of us and we were part of him. That outpouring of affection for Lightfoot in those early years would form the basis for a relationship spanning almost a quarter-century.

There was a bit of luck, too, in being ready when the time was ripe for, if not Lightfoot, then somebody else just exactly like him. Being guided by the best management company in America did not hurt him either.

Whatever the reasons, by the end of 1966, Lightfoot had established himself as the country's national troubadour, the singer of its songs and the embodiment of its consciousness. What could he do next?

What he could do was become even more aggressive and set out to conquer all of North America and even, if only in his own deepest fantasies, the whole world.

Chapter 6

Top of the Pops

The Riverboat gigs were by now a Toronto tradition with an appearance by Lightfoot penned in for each January and June, for a month at a time. It might seem that even two months each year in the same place would be too much, but Lightfoot was becoming a Toronto institution; there was never an empty seat at the Boat, and hundreds more each week stood at the back to hear him.

Markle described a typical Riverboat concert:

They're introduced (The Riverboat proudly presents, etc.) and out they come, bass player John Stockfish, everybody clapping, lead guitar Red Shea (big smile, bushy hair, he's a groove, enthusiastic) clap, clap, clap, then, and the applause is louder, Gordon Lightfoot up front, on the stand, into the red and blue lights, all showbusy, all ready to work.

Now it's nice and quiet, the audience in the dark, waiting expecting, and he starts to sing.

...Quiet again, more music, into "A Minor Ballad," and "Walls," both new tunes, very recent, lights changing, just the three of them, Gord's in good voice, caressing his lyrics.

Just the three of them playing, close to their audience.

Now the lights go all blue and quiet, he begins a ballad, "Softly,"

then on to more tunes, under glowing lights, rocking through
"Rosanna," "Go Go Round," pleasing the crowd with "If You Got
It," "Crossroads." Again, the lights change, hazy through ciga-
rette smoke. And a deep breath, and into a masterpiece... "The
Canadian Railroad Trilogy."
... It's over, the great song is over. Thank you, he says, and off the
stand, sweaty, to recoup. Great applause. Thunder. He owns the
room.
Over, end of set. The people pile out, more people pile in. One set
down, three more to go.

Some of the things Markle noticed arose out of his
relationship with Lightfoot. The newest, the latest, songs
that Lightfoot had written would particularly strike his ears
because they had been largely written in his studio; he had
heard the first tentative attempts at a line or a riff, the
struggle to find some small inspiration for a chorus or a
bridge; he had laughed and cheered when, finally, the
whole thing came together into a finely-crafted pop song.

The close relationship between Lightfoot and his Riverboat audience was another thing Markle perceived and
wrote about. He had noticed it that very first afternoon, in
his studio with the gang from the Pilot, and had watched
Lightfoot nurture it until now he basked in almost idolatrous affection.

Fielder's habit of throwing the audience back onto the
streets and replacing it with a new one after each set did not
escape his sharp eye either. Nor did the fact that Lightfoot
was "all showbusy, ready to work." Privy to the preparation
that went into each public appearance of new work, he saw
the business side of what the audience might have thought
of only as everybody having a good time.

Immediately after the gig at the Boat in January 1967,
Lightfoot took Stockfish and Shea with him to record a
second United Artists album down in Nashville. In Nash-

Lightfoot with Robert Markle in Yorkville, 1967.

Patti and Bernie Fiedler at home, 1966.

ville, he was considered to be a successful out-of-towner. He wasn't one of the boys and he didn't always play by the rules. Nashville producers did not allow you to bring your own band members along with you on a recording date. Why would they? The Nashville cats who played on hundreds of recording dates each year were the very best in the world. To get a bit of the Nashville sound on the album, two good ol' boys in Nashville, Ken Buttrey and Charlie McCoy were added to the basic Lightfoot band.

Up to this time, American country singers had been good to Lightfoot, recording his songs with even more regularity than his fellow folkies. In Nashville, especially under producer Chet Atkins at RCA Victor, there was a movement to sell country acts like Johnny Cash and John D. Laudermilk and Roger Miller as country-folk entertainers, in an attempt to cross over into what was thought to be a more lucrative pop field. It was natural for Lightfoot to foster the relationship by recording his album in Nashville. However, when the album, called *The Way I Feel*, was completed, it did not contain a natural country music hit. If anything, it was even more folk-sounding and less country-sounding than the songs he had earlier written, even with the presence of Buttrey and McCoy on the album.

The Way I Feel, featuring a close-up photo of Lightfoot looking every bit the British "mod" with his Caesar-style new haircut similar to the one sported by Canada's then Minister of Justice, Pierre Trudeau, was a collection of songs forming the core of Lightfoot's concerts at the Riverboat.

In addition to tender love ballads like "Softly" and "The Way I Feel" (recorded for a second time on as many albums), it included the Dylanesque "If You Got It;" the traditional-sounding "A Minor Ballad" and "Home From the Forest;" a charming fable about a country girl mistreated by a big-city musician (Lightfoot himself?) called "Go Go

Round;" and three songs exploring, surely for the first time in the history of English-Canadian pop music history, the meaning and the effect of the vast, white spaces and the dense, green forests that comprise the terror of the Canadian landscape: "Song For A Winter's Night," "Crossroads" and "Canadian Railroad Trilogy." In these three songs Lightfoot had created a singular space for himself among all the other writers and singers vying for the attention of the Canadian public. His reputation as a balladeer of his country would from now on be so secure that he could calmly seek success in the wider field of American pop music without losing his hold on his Canadian audience.

Despite the fact that Lightfoot was trying to lighten his commitments in the Toronto area, he had to return from Nashville for a previously-booked engagement from which he couldn't escape. Having created one tradition with his twice-yearly appearances at the Riverboat, he was now to start another, by playing the first of what would later become the famous Massey Hall concerts. Like all the others to follow, the first Massey Hall concert, on March 31, 1967, was sold out. Extra seats were placed on the stage to accommodate the overflow crowd. He was wildly successful, both with the enthusiastic audience and the critics. The Toronto *Telegram* especially noted his "brilliant creative mind, a mind that is keenly attuned to the human condition and uniquely able to reflect it musically." After the concert there was a wild party at Lightfoot's place to celebrate the success. The after-Massey Hall parties would become another Toronto tradition.

Everyone who was anyone in Toronto's music scene—the singers, the band members, the record company executives, the club owners, the bookers, the agents, the hangers-on and the groupies—all would show up at Lightfoot's parties. The food was good, the booze flowed and the drugs

were plentiful. Music fed all the appetites. Deals and love
affairs were consummated. Angry fights would break out
between the many conflicting overblown egos filling the
house. Through it all, Lightfoot would quietly stride, a beer
bottle in hand, staying away from the main action, shyly
retreating into dark corners and back rooms, until it might
have seemed that he was an uninvited guest, rather than the
host of the affair. Often, a friend like Markle would crash
over for the night, and breakfast the next morning would
be a solemn affair of reminiscences, recriminations and
hangover remedies. One famous party was reputed to have
lasted nine days. If it wasn't exactly life in the fast lane, this
was about as fast as Toronto ever got.

This was the year of Expo '67, a giant year-long party
celebrating Canada's one hundredth birthday. All across
the country, special events and galas were erupting. The
music scene was in overdrive. In a head-long rush to bring
culture to the masses, concert halls and arts centres were
springing up across the land. They all had to be filled with
entertainers. Gordon Lightfoot joined the Festival Canada
tour, a group of entertainers criss-crossing the country by
train in celebration of Canada's birthday. It was another
months-long party. With Shea and Stockfish, he did three
weeks of concerts at the Ontario Pavilion of Expo '67 and,
towards the end of the year, performed at the Quebec
pavilion.

As if to prove that Stephen Leacock was not its only
famous son and that it was not a backwater in twentieth-
century Canadian life, the town of Orillia declared August
5, 1967 to be Gordon Lightfoot Day. The town pulled out
all the stops, with the traditional parade, the presentation of
the newly-traditional Centennial Medal and a pair of
charity concerts, with the proceeds going towards lights for
a new town park.

The relationship between Lightfoot and his home town

of Orillia had become more complicated. If he had once sought nothing more than to shake the dust of Orillia from his cowboy boots, the town itself sought nothing less than to bind Lightfoot to it by showering him with honours and gifts. He was inducted into the Orillia Hall of Fame on that day, joining Leacock and Frost and de la Roche in the pantheon of the gods of Orillia.

In years to come, a courtly dance between Lightfoot and the town would be enacted, a dance within which the town would attempt to embrace Lightfoot in return for the donation of his time and talent to a series of civic events and charitable occasions, while Lightfoot would politely resist the civic embrace save on the most rare of occasions.

In June, he did his month-long gig at the Riverboat one more time. It must have seemed by now that all the years were becoming the same, all the bestsellers and awards and concerts were blurring into a recognizable pattern, a pattern that can deaden the soul, that can waste the mind and bloat the body. Not surprisingly, Lightfoot was responding by slipping further into heavy drinking and finding relief from the arguments at home by repeated adulteries. However, compared to many other pop stars who, when faced with the rigours of the road and the demands of a public greedy for every excess, drive themselves into ever-increasing frenzies of self-destruction, Lightfoot somehow managed to balance all the elements of his life, if not expertly, at least competently. His songwriting continued to be strong, and his public appearances were improving, even sometimes showing a light deftness of touch missing in his earlier, more strained concerts.

But as the year zoomed by, with only the names of the towns changing and the faces of the audience looking exactly the same everywhere he went, the honours and the awards continued to arrive. His Nashville album, *The Way I Feel*, hit the Number One spot on the Canadian charts in mid-summer. "Go Go Round" went gold. He won the music industry's MIDEM award for being the bestselling Canadian recording artist in 1966-67. Winning that award is less important than making all the money that comes in for the same reason.

Continuing what was becoming an autumn tradition, he went back to New York in December to record what was to become his most successful album yet. He called it *Did She Mention My Name?* Moving away from the Nashville sound which had not seemed to reap any rewards the previous year, he tried a more orchestral sound, using a string section. He also changed producers. His new producer was John Simon, who had previously produced Dylan, The Band and Leonard Cohen.

With nationalist fervour in white heat during that year of Canada's centennial, Lightfoot had responded with his recording of "Canadian Railroad Trilogy," a six-minute tribute to the men who had created the Canadian Pacific Railroad in the nineteenth century. Nowhere in the land of that centennial year could you go without hearing that song, or hearing about that song. It became a second national anthem, sung by a hundred other folk groups and a thousand school choral groups, until it seemed that Gordon Lightfoot himself held the key to unlocking the unconscious of a whole country. It was far too long to be released as a pop single, yet in that year you could hardly find a single Canadian who could not at least hum its melody and sing a snatch of its many verses.

Just as Woody Guthrie had done for American folk song in creating a mythology of common folk united in a struggle for their daily bread and a measure of human dignity, and like Gilles Vigneault was doing in Quebec folk song by creating a musical landscape for the aspirations of a people to form their own nation, Lightfoot was creating a common mythology for English Canada and expressing a collective history for a people who felt they did not even have a history except as a footnote to the American experience.

Through that one song, and through the appeal it had in all parts of the country and to people in all circumstances of life, Lightfoot had moved from being a troubadour only for the hip, the intellectual, the stoned, to becoming a singer of the consciousness of a nation. This connection with a whole population, when strengthened and deepened through repetition and through new works, would become the basis of an unyielding bond that would connect Lightfoot and his audience through the turmoils and tribulations of the next two decades.

Ironically, Canadians were now bonded to a man who was obsessed with becoming an American star. He wanted to make it in the States.

In the sixties, musicians throughout the world considered the streets of America to be paved with gold records, and the quest for Number One on the American charts took on the aura of a mythical quest. Like crusaders of an earlier time, these musicians—armed with guitar, bass and drums—left their homeland to conquer a foreign land, the mythical land of the Americas, in search of their own holy grail—a plaque containing a replica of their record which had sold a million copies (at a dollar a disc) in the United States, a plaque called a Gold Record.

Ironically, like the very gold standard upon which the honour is based, the Gold Record today has been devalued, requiring sales of only 502,000 copies (at today's record prices, still signifying a million dollars in sales) to be replaced by a more modern standard, called a Platinum Record.

By the end of 1967, having conquered his homeland of Canada, Gordon Lightfoot wanted all of America at his feet, he wanted the tangible proof that he was as good as anyone in the U.S., he wanted his million-selling Gold

Record. He would spend years on this quest, until no one could deny its fulfillment. But to achieve his desires, he would be forced to make wrenching changes in both his business life and his personal life.

He began a two-year long battle with the Grossman organization over the question of whether Lightfoot even had the possibility of making it in the United States. Lightfoot was convinced that, by making the right career moves, he could easily break into the American Top Forty. Grossman wasn't so sure. He felt that perhaps Lightfoot should be content with his Canadian success, and forget about competing with Dylan and Joan Baez and the new folk-rock groups.

Lightfoot's record sales in the U.S. certainly bore out Grossman's theory. His first album had sold only a disappointing twenty thousand units, a far cry from the expectations after the exhilaration of the recording session in late 1964. His second record sold a bit better but both were consigned to the delete bins shortly after release. Grossman felt that there was something so understated, so Canadian, perhaps, about Lightfoot's singing that he could never fulfil the American audience's demand for passionate hysteria in their pop heroes. His management plans for Lightfoot involved continuing to feed his songs to American singers and to present Lightfoot in small, intimate clubs where his folksy charm could win over a tiny group who would remain loyal over the years. These plans would have forever doomed Lightfoot to the margins of pop music history.

Lightfoot disagreed. He could see no vast differences between the audiences in Detroit and New York and the audiences in Toronto and Vancouver. If he could please the one, he should be able to win over the other. He felt that the reason his first two albums had not sold well in the United States was because they had not been correctly promoted by United Artists. He was proud of his albums and bitterly disappointed in their poor sales. He also felt that Grossman's concentration on the Canadian market, where Lightfoot was already a star, was an easier route than pushing the American market and a route that would ultimately doom him to the status of a provincial non-entity.

He began formulating his own plan to make it in the States. Key to the plan was his decision to fulfil his contractual commitment to both United Artists and the Grossman organization, then dump them both at the earliest opportunity. And he would deliberately set out to create a hit song in America.

The subject of his first attempt at the hit arose out of his own pain at what was happening in America. In those closing years of the sixties, as Richard Nixon began his assault on the presidency of the United States, as the Democratic Party was tearing itself apart over its Vietnam war policy, as hundreds of thousands of Americans took to the streets to protest against that ugly war, the inner cities throughout the country erupted into anarchy and destruction to the chant of "Burn, Baby, Burn." There was a fierce anger in the air, an anger no less on the Right than it was on the Left. Beginning in the Watts ghetto of Los Angeles, city after city pitted its poor, its unemployed, its blacks, against the police, the National Guard, the whites. In July of 1967, the city of Detroit had erupted in looting and burning. The uprising was brutally quashed, with scores of rioters left dead on the streets. Americans, and people throughout the world, looked on with horror as America seemed hell-bent on destroying itself. The government promised firmness and repression, but Americans had already lost faith in their government and were eager to replace it with another, even more firm and repressive.

Detroit had a special fascination for Lightfoot. He

Black Day in July, Detroit, 1967. (Photo by Philip Webb, courtesy of the Detroit *News*)

thought of it as a second home and it truly made his heart ache when it erupted into flames. In anger and in sadness, he wrote a protest song he called "Black Day in July." The song was filled with pain and bitterness. If it can be said that Lightfoot was deliberately seeking access to the American pop charts, it must also be admitted that the chosen vehicle was a heartfelt plea for an end to violence and a vivid description of the horrors of urban anarchy. "Black Day in July" stands in Lightfoot's repertoire as the most overtly political song he has ever written, perhaps because the burning of Detroit was the one political event in America which touched him most deeply.

Lightfoot began using the song in his concerts and sang it on an hour-long CBC television special in March of 1968. The record he released quickly rose to the top of the Canadian charts, an anomaly among the raucous rock songs surrounding it on the radio and in the jukeboxes.

In the United States, Lightfoot's hopes of reaching a wide American audience were quickly dashed. All across the country, the major AM radio stations refused to play the song. This was an act of overt political self-censorship, although the song itself could hardly be considered a call to arms. For whatever the reasons, and some radio stations no doubt acted in a desire to quell the flames of dissent rather than to fan them, the ban on the record destroyed Lightfoot's hopes of a major hit. Even CKLW in Windsor, which had helped propel the song to the top of the Canadian charts, soon removed it from its playlist—an acknowledgement of the sensibilities of its listeners across the river in Detroit, perhaps. The failure of United Artists to break the boycott of the record in America only served to fuel Lightfoot's bitterness at their ineffectiveness.

Lightfoot no longer cares for "Black Day in July," saying he now feels uncomfortable that he once considered himself qualified to comment on the problems of another country. He says that he now does not like any of his songs which might be described as "protest music."

For the third year in a row, Lightfoot continued the by now predictable pattern of concert appearances, tours and record releases. If the failure of "Black Day in July" rankled him, he did not show it, throwing himself into his work. The year 1968 was more of the same: a tour of England, an appearance on the Johnny Cash television show, two more concerts at Massey Hall, a new album recorded in Mount Juliet, Tennessee, called *Back Here on Earth*, a new Canadian hit single with his song "Bitter Green," an award for Best Singer (Male), and another trophy to signify over a million dollars of record sales in Canada. But all the parties, all the booze, all the women, all the dope which came with these achievements still could not ease the hurt that he was not considered seriously in America.

Lightfoot still owed United Artists one more album on his contract. During 1968, he had written a large body of new songs, many of them during his tour of Britain early in the year. He describes writing the album *Back Here on Earth* in a hotel room in London, England. He says, "I hardly left the room except to go out and have a drink. I'd go to sleep at midnight, get up at seven and write straight through to midnight." The isolation of being in England has helped him create new works at least three times in his career; on another occasion, he wrote a series of new songs while in a train compartment travelling through the English country- side. But he was damned if he was going to give these songs to a record company which was going to waste them.

So, for his last UA release, he decided to record a live album of older songs. It was a clever ploy, allowing him to approach a new company with a stack of new material in hand. By March of 1969, the Massey Hall concerts had become a yearly ritual in Toronto, with additional shows being added each year to accommodate the seemingly never-ending overflow of fans who filled the hall for each concert. That year, the concerts had been expanded to four shows and Lightfoot taped them all. The resulting live album, called *Sunday Concert*, fulfilled Lightfoot's obligations to United Artists.

In May of that year, Lightfoot demanded, and received, his release from UA and announced that he had formed his own production company, called Early Morning Productions, named after his first songwriting success. He hired Al Mair, a businessman and record executive for the Compo Company, as his general manager. Lightfoot had plans for Early Morning Productions. One day, he hoped, it would be the funnel for all of his business activities and there would be no need for a middle man such as Grossman. By eliminating the middle man, he would also make more money, a point not lost on Lightfoot who was, by now, becoming much more aware of how the music business really worked.

In an effort to keep control over his recorded material, Lightfoot offered United Artists a half-million dollars for the rights to the music he had recorded for them. Perhaps aware that the ultimate value of the songs was much more that, the record company refused his offer. In future years, they would re-release the old material, infuriating Lightfoot who then was forced to compete with his earlier self.

Grossman's contract with Lightfoot did not run out until the end of 1970. Grossman was considered to be the canniest of American managers. Through the previous two years, he had followed what he felt was the correct management path for a singer like Lightfoot. He had kept his American bookings small but prestigious. Like Lightfoot, he had waited for that first hit single to emerge from an album, even if he felt that Lightfoot would never make it in America. But now, with Lightfoot on the free market for a recording contract, he could shop him around and squeeze the market for every penny.

As a last gesture to prove his worth as a manager (and perhaps, it must be admitted, to ensure that he would receive his commission on any new record deal), Grossman obtained for Lightfoot an almost unheard of recording contract with Warner Brothers-Reprise, one of the new conglomerates that were squeezing the smaller record labels off the market. The contract called for an advance of a million dollars (although such huge figures are often clouded in restrictions, being more of a public relations gesture to signify the importance of the artist being signed than a firm commitment to deposit a cheque the next day). In the case of the Warner Brothers contract, the money was to be spread over five years. It was a contract generous enough to stir feelings of the utmost envy in the American folk scene. Lightfoot's obligation in return was to make a lot of hit records for Warner Brothers.

Admitting defeat against Lightfoot's intransigence and stubbornness, Grossman booked him more frequently in the U.S. during 1969 in an attempt to expand his audience. He was setting Lightfoot up for his assault on the American consciousness, even if he wouldn't be along for the ride.

Immediately following the signing of the lucrative contract, Lightfoot began recording the songs he had written but had kept away from United Artists. He used American folk-rockers John Sebastian and Randy Newman and guitar wizard Ry Cooder to add a rougher-edged texture to his material.

One of the first songs he recorded was intended to be the first single from the album. It was called "Me and Bobby McGee," written by Kris Kristofferson. Lightfoot had heard a tape of Kristofferson songs the previous summer while he was in Nashville taping a segment of the *Johnny Cash Show*, and had been impressed with all of the songs, but especially with "Me and Bobby McGee," which he felt particularly suited his own singing style.

Kristofferson had achieved a small success on the coffee-house circuit but had not yet succeeded in convincing Nashville that he was a bona-fide country writer and singer. Perhaps that was because such songs as "Blame It On The Stones" were attacks on middle-American morality or because others, such as "Help Me Make It Through The Night," were unabashedly sexual in nature, and the Nashville powers were reluctant to accept the sexual revolution that was changing America. Or perhaps it was simply that the excruciatingly literate lyrics of the Rhodes Scholar Kristofferson couldn't be fathomed by the good 'ol boys in Nashville.

In the song "Me and Bobby McGee," Lightfoot felt he had found his ticket to the Top Ten in America and he was willing to bend his rules against singing other people's songs. However, Kristofferson had his own problems to take care of.

Country singer Roger Miller had also expressed interest in putting out the song as a country single. Miller was hot stuff in Nashville, the winner of a Grammy award and the singer of such Top-Ten crossover hits as "King of the Road" and "England Swings." To have Roger Miller record one of your songs would indicate acceptance by the Nashville establishment.

So Kristofferson phoned Lightfoot, requesting that he postpone his plans to release "Me and Bobby McGee" in favour of Miller's version. Reluctantly, Lightfoot agreed, including it on his new album and singing it for years at his concerts, but delaying its release as a single.

In the event, Kristofferson had made the correct decision for his own career. Miller's version was a big country hit, and when female country singer Sammi Smith recorded "Help Me Make It Through the Night," and that record was an even bigger hit, Kristofferson's career in Nashville was assured. He later made a second career for himself in

Ronnie Hawkins, Lightfoot and Kris Kristofferson performing "Me and Bobby McGee" at the Nickelodeon in 1971.

Lightfoot joins a stripper on the dance floor at the Nickelodeon.

Hollywood, starring in such films as *Cisco Pike* and *A Star is Born.*

As for Lightfoot, this was the second time in as many years that he had seen his hopes for an American hit dashed. Maybe he should have released it anyway, for later Janis Joplin recorded a version that outsold Miller's tenfold. But perhaps it was not a totally unwise move on Lightfoot's part, since his career might have turned out differently had he made his first major impact on America with someone else's song.

One distinctive version of this song was later performed when Ronnie Hawkins invited Lightfoot and Kris Kristofferson to join him onstage at the Nickelodeon, where they all three contributed to a ragged version of "Me and Bobby McGee." Hawkins joked, "It took me two hundred dollars worth of dope to get these guys to do this." During the raucous evening, Lightfoot joined a bikini-clad stripper from nearby Lori Lane's Le Strip club on the Nickelodeon's dance floor and did his own version of a striptease.

In any case, he did not get his American hit. He continued touring in both Canada and the United States. In May of 1970, he was once more back in Toronto at Massey Hall. He could use the occasion to visit with Brita and Fred and Ingrid. He and Brita could talk about getting a permanent separation.

In ongoing attempts to find domestic harmony (and increase the family assets), the Lightfoots had bought a succession of new and ever larger homes. From the basement apartment on Arlington, to the duplex on Farnham, to a bigger house a few streets away on Poplar Plains Road, they had finally settled into a large house at the corner of Blythwood Road and Mount Pleasant in North Toronto. But, as if to signify to the world the permanence in his own mind of their separation, Lightfoot also rented an apartment on the twenty-eighth floor of a downtown

At home, on Poplar Plains.

(Photo by Daniel Kramer, courtesy of Lightfoot)

high-rise. He began living the life of the carefree bachelor inviting a succession of young ladies to share his apartment, for at least a little while.

By coincidence, while visiting Bernie Fiedler one evening, he ran into Cathy Smith once again. They reminisced about old times and rekindled their affair.

Lightfoot had just completed another successful Massey Hall gig and his new album had been released by Warner Brothers to kind reviews and the expectation of major sales. To celebrate his success, he invited Cathy to a night on the town. By choosing not to celebrate with Brita, Lightfoot had made a calculated and deliberate decision.

He took her to Toronto's most exclusive and expensive restaurant, Winston's. Winston's generally catered more to the likes of John Turner and Ontario Premier William Davis than to musicians and their groupies. However, by ordering a three-hundred-dollar bottle of wine, Lightfoot announced his status as a nouveau-millionaire and the staff of Winston's were suitably obsequious.

Lightfoot invited Cathy, who had wisely given up Tracy Lee for adoption some time earlier, to move into his twenty-eighth-floor apartment and she eagerly agreed. She has described the apartment as "a total bachelor fantasy," with deep pile rugs, oversized furniture, an aquarium and a secret spring-loaded top to the coffee table to hide the marijuana stash. The apartment's decor ran to red flocked wallpaper, deep gold velvet couches, a red-and-purple draped doorway, Tiffany lamps, Eskimo carvings and paintings on the wall, including a Markle portrait. If such a place fulfilled Lightfoot's deepest fantasies of living the ultimate pop star's life, it is no wonder that he would be so discontented sharing a life with a wife and children to make demands on his time and his fantasies. His most ardent fans, many of whom were making a fetish of challenging and rejecting the middle-class comfort of their parents' home, would have been totally perplexed had they known about the luxurious high-rise apartment they had helped to pay for each time they bought an album or attended a concert. They still saw Lightfoot as a wandering troubadour, as one of their spokesmen in a world that was corrupt, as one whose magic could somehow destroy that corruption and replace it with the grace of beauty and gentleness. The trouble with that vision of Lightfoot was that it was not, and never had been, true.

For Lightfoot, such arguments by his audience would have been dismissed out of hand. He did not feel he owed his audience anything beyond a good concert and a new song every once in a while. He had worked hard to get where he was, he had struggled and schemed and denied himself security and love and peace to achieve the triumphs he now enjoyed. Who could deny him the small luxury of his bachelor fantasy?

That summer of 1970, while he lived with Cathy Smith, he was a perplexed and worried man. He made simultaneous overtures to his wife for a reconciliation and a permanent separation leading to divorce. He knew he wasn't terribly happy, but he wasn't sure which way would lead to happiness. His new album, once again, was selling far below expectations; six months after its release, it had sold only 150,000 copies.

It looked like, once again, his dreams were crumbling. Another minor hit on the Canadian charts would no longer please him. He spent the summer alternately trying to write new songs and revelling in his new romance, fuelling that romantic affair with copious amounts of the best food, wine and dope that lovers everywhere use as aphrodisiac.

In August, he made two decisions. He would get away from all the turmoil and regret by going along with a friend from Ottawa, Michael Landry, and a couple of buddies on a canoeing trip up the Rupert River in Northern Quebec.

Upon his return he would go back to Brita and try once more to see if he could make a marriage out of the shambles his love life had become.

The canoe trip was as perfect as only a canoe trip mounted with enough money to get into the most isolated parts of northern Canada can be. It was so successful that a yearly canoe trip has been a part of Lightfoot's admittedly rigid schedule ever since. These canoe trips are not the drinking binges other Canadian canoeing and fishing trips often become; this is serious canoeing, with rapids to shoot, isolation and loneliness to overcome and, ultimately, the blessed release from the constant expectations and demands of both the private and the public parts of life. If an annual canoe trip can be seen as the epitome of male Canadians' fantasies, it is also a viably therapeutic method of achieving a self-cleansing and a self-redemption. On his canoeing expeditions, Lightfoot has found one way of coping with what his life has become. It is the one time each year he can feel pure and free.

Before leaving, Lightfoot had informed Cathy of his decision to return to Brita, and she was in the mood for revenge. She moved out of Lightfoot's apartment and began seeing Brian Good.

Lightfoot and Brian Good had been friends since the early days of the Yorkville folk scene. Good had played on Lightfoot's albums, and Lightfoot contributed songs and liner notes to the albums of the Good Brothers, the country group fronted by Brian and his brother Dave. Lightfoot had introduced Cathy and Brian. Cathy's and Brian's affair lasted a few weeks, until the Good Brothers left town to perform in the San Francisco area.

After his canoe trip, Lightfoot moved back in with Brita and the kids. It didn't work out. Brita had calculated that, since their marriage, Lightfoot had lived at home only about one-third of the time. She threw his infidelities into

Making bannock on a canoe trip down the Kazan River.

On a canoeing expedition to Great Slave Lake, in 1985.

his face. He countered that she only wanted to shackle him to her, that she was only interested in his money. Anger and bitterness and, according to Brita, physical violence erupted.

They decided that, this time, they would separate for good. Brita could sue him for divorce; he would not contest.

He moved back into his apartment. Things were not working out. He had finally, after much soul-searching, decided to return to Brita and that plan had exploded in his face. Perhaps, unconsciously, he had even intended it to happen that way. And his new album still wasn't selling. His new relationship with Warner Brothers was in a shambles.

When Cathy returned to the apartment, Lightfoot angrily confronted her with her infidelity with Good. She defended herself, asking why it was all right for him to return to his wife, but objectionable that she find a new lover. He called her a slut and threw her out of the apartment. Cathy hitchhiked to San Francisco to see the Good Brothers.

Cathy did have a point: like most musicians and like males everywhere, Lightfoot was demanding the social code of the double standard, whereby his sexual conduct was to be beyond reproach but any woman with whom he was having a relationship would have to maintain the strictest standards of sexual fidelity. With Cathy Smith, and with an increasingly large number of women at the end of the sixties, you could not demand such a code. After all, this is the woman about whom the most frequently repeated anecdote concerns the time in a restaurant singer Dan Hill asked if he could eat one of her potato chips. Her reply was, "If I give you one do we get to fuck later?" Definitely not a woman to whom you could ever apply the double standard. For the moment, at least, the affair was over.

Sometimes the hits and misses of a musical career hinge on coincidence and fluke. Lightfoot had spent the summer worrying about the failure of his album. Then, in the fall of 1970, a disc jockey in Seattle, Washington began playing a cut entitled, "If You Could Read My Mind." The radio audience responded with demands for the single and repeated requests for the song on the air. Unfortunately, the song wasn't available as a single. That should have been the end of the story.

However, Warner Brothers, as if to prove to Lightfoot that they knew how to make a hit record and that he had made the smart move in leaving United Artists, flexed its muscles and proved its hit-making power.

Learning of the action in Seattle, the record company immediately released "If You Could Read My Mind" as a single and began actively promoting it. Further, it recalled all copies of the album, called *Sit Down Young Stranger*, and re-issued it under the new title, *If You Could Read My Mind*. It worked! Suddenly, Lightfoot had his American hit record. Both the album and the single roared to the top of the charts. The single sold almost a million copies and Lightfoot was close to obtaining his first American gold single.

That there was an element of fluke in the fact that the song first broke in Seattle cannot be denied. Nor can it be denied that, presented with that fluke, Warner Brothers did everything that can be asked of a record company to ensure that a regional favourite would become a national bestseller.

In December 1970, Lightfoot made one of his rare benefit performances back in Orillia, raising twenty-six hundred dollars to build a new dormitory at the YMCA Breezy Point Camp for Boys. He didn't demand a fee: "It sounded sort of crazy to be talking about money in a seven-hundred-seat auditorium in your own home town." The town officials expressed their gratitude when Mayor David Brown presented him with the first key to the city ever presented.

At the end of that year, Lightfoot's life reflected its usual

Posing in 1967.

On the Johnny Cash Show, *1970.*

contradictions and turmoils. He had turned the corner on many aspects of his past life. He had abandoned his record label to find a new one. His relationship with his manager had come to an end. He was officially separated from his wife and children. His girlfriend had left him. He was no longer speaking to one of his best friends.

But he had his American hit. He had finally, after all the years of struggle, reached the top of the pops.

Over the next decade, he would painfully discover that getting to the top was the easy part. Staying there would be incomparably more difficult.

Chapter 7

Apache Dancing

At first, having that coveted hit record in America did not change Lightfoot's life at all. He was too busy to luxuriate in it. He had concert engagements booked for months ahead, and he was spending the winter and spring in Nashville writing and recording his next album, to be called *Summer Side of Life*. The album had no obvious hit material and, while his new status as a chart-topper ensured it would sell fairly well, it failed to match the sales of *If You Could Read My Mind*.

Immediately after completing the album, he flew back to Toronto for another series of Massey Hall concerts, which once again were sold out and received glowing reviews.

In the spring of 1971, the Canadian government's regulating body for broadcasting, the Canadian Radio-Television Commission, instituted new rules for Canadian content on the radio which would strongly boost Lightfoot's already-high profile in Canada.

Headed by cultural bureaucrat Pierre Juneau, the CRTC was, in the early seventies, strongly influenced by two seemingly conflicting theories: one was a fervent Canadian cultural nationalism, the other the communications and media concepts of Professor Marshall McLuhan, of the University of Toronto.

One theory of McLuhan's, which had a major impact on the public, academics and bureaucrats, had to do with what he called "the global village." In his books *The Gutenberg Galaxy* and *Understanding Media,* McLuhan argued that modern mass communications had shrunk nation-states to the status of one world-wide village, wherein everybody was privy to the most intimate secrets of everybody else and where a seemingly unimportant event in one part of the village affected everybody else, no matter how widely separated by geography people were.

The instruments of this globe-shrinking, argued McLuhan, were radio, television and computers. His arguments held a common-sense appeal even to the general public, although his more complex theories were sometimes dismissed as ivory tower intellectualism. The Vietnam War, which affected the politics of not only Vietnam and the U.S.A., but also the Soviet Union, China, Europe, and even Canada, and the simultaneous student uprisings and counter-culture movements in all parts of the world (save the Communist states), seemed to validate McLuhan's reasoning.

In Canada, communications policies had become, especially after the creation of the CBC in the 1930s, an integral part of government planning, in a McLuhanesque effort to unite the far-flung regions of the country within a unified broadcasting system. What highways and railroads could not do, transmitters and electrical wires were accomplishing. Canada embraced the communications revolution.

This revolution in communications created social effects which were not always foreseen or beneficial, according to McLuhan. His theories were often seen by communications specialists, however, only as explanations of the inevitable and, ultimately, the desirable.

In the late sixties, with the creation of communications satellites capable of transmitting live television throughout the world, and with the development of a system of cable transmission of television signals far beyond the normal broadcasting power of a television station, television assumed the power of transcending national boundaries. Where armies and mercenaries could not invade, television could.

For Canada, eager proponent of communications innovation, the development of cable television posed special problems. In theory, cable runs two ways and, if American television stations hundred of miles from the border could now transmit into Canada, Canadian stations could also be cabled into the heartland of America. The law of supply and demand nullified this theory, of course, for while Canadians were eager to expand the number of television stations available to them by importing American transmissions, Americans had no interest in watching Canadian television which, after all, consists mainly of American shows and Canadian shows designed to imitate American shows. In practice, the cable runs only one way.

The planners at the CRTC, given the task of regulating the new technology, were aware of the demand for American programming. They were also aware of the possibility that, having once entered the market, the Americans could begin to unfairly compete for the advertising dollars which formed the base of commercial broadcasting. So, while embracing the McLuhan theories which described the global village wired by technology, they imposed restrictions on cable operators, forcing them to create local programming. They were attempting to pacify critics of cable technology by forcing cable operators to spend some part of their profits locally in their community. They might have read McLuhan further, for he also pointed out that neither language, culture, nor national policy were sufficient resources with which to battle the effects of the global communications revolution, especially if that revolution was understood in national, rather than global, terms.

In its decision regarding the future of the cable television industry, the CRTC had thus come down in favour of the global village. When it created new policies regarding radio broadcasting, it did the reverse and imposed strict rules of nationalist intent. Perhaps this was because radio was an older broadcasting medium and less important in the minds of the CRTC planners. Perhaps it was an attempt to balance its policies and to appease the demands of cultural nationalists who correctly pointed out the lack of Canadian control over the contents of the records played on Canadian radio and the films screened in Canadian theatres. The CRTC had no mandate to impose film policy but it could revolutionize radio programming.

Thus, over the anguished objections of radio station owners across the country who feared that audiences would diminish if they played less American music, the CRTC forced all stations to carry a minimum of 30 percent Canadian content. The rules were fairly rigid, although they allowed singers and composers like Robert Goulet and Paul Anka, who had long ago abandoned their country for the warmer climate and larger paycheques of the United States, to be classified as Canadians for the purpose of the regulations.

For the most part, the Canadian recording industry was pleased. Some predicted an unprecedented outpouring of Canadian music which would sweep the country and even the world. Others gloomily predicted that only established stars would benefit from the rules.

For a long time, the pessimistic view seemed to be validated. Faced with the task of finding enough music that qualified as Canadian content, many programmers turned to the first resource at hand: Gordon Lightfoot records.

If Lightfoot's music had already been a staple of radio programming in Canada for a half-decade, it now seemed as if every second recording made by a Canadian was by

Lightfoot. He was the staple of country programming, of middle-of-the-road programming and of pop programming. During those early years of the seventies, it sometimes seemed that Lightfoot and, to a lesser degree, singer Anne Murray were dividing between them the time allotted for the 30 percent of Canadian records required by law.

There are those who would argue that it was only because of the CRTC regulations that Lightfoot and Murray managed to survive as long as they both have, the implication being that only stern government regulations could force Canadians to listen to their music. This argument ignores the fact that both these singers enjoyed international acclaim at the same time as their music was being force-fed to Canadian listeners.

Lightfoot himself has been ambivalent about the effects of the CRTC ruling on his career. He once told Markle, "The CRTC did absolutely nothing for me, I don't need it and I don't like it...I really dig this country, but I'm not going to bring out any flags. I'm an entertainer, I'm in the music business." But, as the astute businessman he was more and more becoming, he could not help but be aware of the increasing songwriter's royalties which were flowing to him because of Canadian content.

With the success of "If You Could Read My Mind," Lightfoot's engagements in the United States and in Europe increased dramatically. He had by now forever left the small coffeehouse circuit, playing to packed houses in concert houses seating from several hundred to several thousand people. He hadn't needed the CRTC decision to fuel his career, although the decision did add many more dollars to his already-deep coffers since the royalty paid for a song on the radio is payable to the composer, and Lightfoot had composed all of his own hit songs.

The next year, Lightfoot and Murray would combine for

a one-two punch against their critics when she recorded Lightfoot's song "Cotton Jenny," and it immediately became another international Number One hit.

Cathy Smith was now travelling with Lightfoot on the road. Their relationship remained tumultuous. They decided to leave Toronto and become country squires on a farm north of Toronto, near the town of Aurora. Lightfoot's drinking had only increased with each success and, combined with the numerous infidelities committed by both of them, led to bitter rages of jealousy and torment. Lightfoot would taunt Cathy with the number of groupies he had had on a particular weekend (the number was always nine), and she would respond with boasts about her other lovers, such as Jack Nicholson and Brian Good.

According to Cathy, during one fight Lightfoot hit her so hard he broke her cheekbone. Lightfoot does not remember the incident the same way. While admitting that violence played a part in their relationship, he denies that he broke her cheekbone. "We were arguing and she over-reacted, spinning around and hitting her cheek against the mantelpiece of the fireplace. I didn't hit her; she caused the accident herself," he says.

Lightfoot left to go on tour. Upon discovering her cheekbone was broken, Cathy informed him by telephone. Filled with remorse, he flew her to Vancouver, paid for her plastic surgery and took her on a vacation to Hawaii.

Cathy also asserts in her autobiography that during one fight Lightfoot pushed her face into a toilet bowl. Reminded of the incident, he treats it lightly with a bit of a twinkle in his eye. "It was a clean toilet bowl," he drawls. "If there was anything in it besides water I never would have done that." His reply is so dead-pan it is hard to tell if he is making a joke or not.

But even the tranquil serenity of a holiday in Hawaii could not mend the troubled affair. According to Cathy,

With Anne Murray backstage at Centennial Auditorium in Saskatoon in 1987.

At Massey Hall, May 1970.

during an argument over her casual attitude towards drugs (a conviction on a drugs charge could mean that Lightfoot would never again be able to work in the United States) Lightfoot lifted her over the railing of their twenty-first-storey hotel balcony as if to hurl her to the beach below. Only the intercession of a security guard calmed down the fight.

Lightfoot denies that the incident ever occurred. "That never happened, not to my knowledge," he asserts. He argues that her story is full of holes. "We both drank, but we hardly did any drugs at all. Cathy got into drugs later, after we had split up. That incident never happened."

Asked to explain why there was so much violence between them, Lightfoot says it was because of "infidelities and jealousies. Both of us were unfaithful to each other and both of us were wildly jealous of each other. I was sometimes crazy with jealousy." It is an irony: two people in love with each other, both insanely jealous of each other, yet neither one of them able to make the commitment to faithfulness which might have saved the relationship.

Clearly their relationship was speeding towards disaster. But, as he had during his troubled relationship with Brita, Lightfoot allowed it to continue along its tortuous route. If he was always reluctant to start a long-term love affair, he was equally reluctant to end one, even when it was clear to everybody concerned that the best days had long passed.

Lightfoot became more involved in the battle with his old record company, United Artists. When he had left them, his offer to buy the rights to all his old material had been refused. Now, with the success of "If You Could Read My Mind," UA had re-released his hits as *The Best of Gordon Lightfoot*. For years, they would continue to re-package the same songs under different titles: *Classic Lightfoot, The Very Best of Gordon Lightfoot (Vols. I and II)* and *A Lightfoot Collection*.

Lightfoot was enraged but United Artists did have the legal right to re-issues. He had no say in the matter. In his concert appearances, he would beg his audience to boycott the re-issues in favour of his new material. In 1975, he would counter by re-recording the old songs and combining them with his newer hits and release the "official" greatest hits package, called *Gord's Gold*. For the moment, hurt and resentful, he could do nothing. The incident, however, did quicken his resolve to enlarge the activities of Early Morning Productions until it would control all aspects of his music. He was now convinced he knew better than anyone what was the best for Lightfoot. Time has not proven him wrong.

Once he had his American hit record and a production company dedicated to furthering every aspect of his career, Lightfoot seemed content to set his energy level at cruise control. Already a creature of habit—the Riverboat appearances, the Massey Hall concerts, the recording session, and the canoeing trip anchoring his yearly schedule with fixed regularity—his musical output for the rest of his career would be more of the same, and still more of the same. Every once in a while, as if to prevent the critics and his audience from nodding off in stupefaction at the relentless familiarity of the new songs which all sounded vaguely like the old songs, he would pull out an odd surprise: another popular hit, a slight change of musical direction, an attempt at acting in a feature film.

The attempt to be a gentleman farmer with Cathy having failed, Lightfoot purchased a distinguished mansion on Bin-Scarth Road in Toronto's upper-class Rosedale neighbourhood. Cathy took up residence on the isolated third floor. Feeling more and more shut out of Lightfoot's life, she often left the big house in Rosedale to stay with friends, and had a brief affair with yet another member of The Band, Richard Manuel.

In early 1972, Lightfoot was faced with a totally unexpected revelation: he was not a well man.

During 1971, he had been bothered by earaches and a
ringing in his ears. Like many people afraid of finding out
the medical truth, he shrugged off the symptoms of illness,
hoping for them to pass. But, by the beginning of the next
year, he could no longer shrug off his discomfort. During
one of his annual Massey Hall concerts, the left side of his
face became numb, he was unable to blink one eye, and he
lost partial use of his mouth. He was filled with terror,
afraid that his career was over.

Fortunately, Dr. Bill Goodman, Lightfoot's personal
physician, was in the Massey Hall audience that night and
he came backstage during intermission to examine his
patient.

He asked Lightfoot to raise his eyebrows. He could only
raise one. The doctor correctly diagnosed the illness as
Bell's Palsy, a degenerative disease of the nerves feeding the
facial muscles, which causes partial or complete paralysis.
He sent out for eight capsules of cortisone, to enable
Lightfoot to finish the concert.

The next day, he sent Lightfoot to Mount Sinai hospital
for three electric shock treatments to stimulate the nerve
muscles to return to life. The treatment was only partially
successful. Dr. Goodman advised Lightfoot to cancel all his
engagements for at least three months.

Feeling vulnerable that his career could easily be over,
Lightfoot followed the advice of his doctor. He cancelled
his schedule for several months in order to recuperate and
began using the prescription drugs which eventually re-
stored his facilities almost to normal. The three months of
recuperation were tormenting. Because he could not close
one eye, he had to sleep with an eye patch on. He could
hardly talk. He has admitted that, at night, he would cry
himself to sleep, wondering if he would ever get better.

Luckily, he did improve. Today he has recovered virtually all the use of his facial muscles. If you look at him, even scrutinize him closely, you would never guess he had once been so debilitated.

With the disease under control by August 1972, he nevertheless began work on a new album at the RCA Victor studios in Toronto. He had no desire to fall ill in the strange environment of New York or Nashville.

He called the album *Old Dan's Records* after one of the cuts. He had written that song after overhearing by chance a patron at a Ronnie Hawkins concert murmur, "I love those old dance records." Intrigued by the phrase, Lightfoot toyed with it late at night, emerging with a song about an old man's collection of 78 RPM discs, "Old Dan's Records."

One song from the album, "Can't Depend on Love," became a Canadian hit, while another, "You Are What I Am," did well in the States. Despite his health problems, and despite his turbulent personal life, his popular appeal was continuing to increase.

The medication he was taking for the Bell's Palsy, and the increasing alcohol consumption—due, in part, to his depression over his health—combined to make him even more violent and uncommunicative. Like a career soldier who can combine a lifelong alcoholism with a spotless military record by dint of dedication and iron will, Lightfoot never allowed his drinking to interfere with his public appearances or his recording sessions. Nobody in his audience had the slightest inkling that he had a drinking problem. It is probably fair to say, however, that many of the reviews of his concerts which complained of a certain listlessness and lack of communication may have unwittingly perceived the results of his heavy drinking.

By the spring of 1973, the Massey Hall concerts had irrevocably replaced the Riverboat appearances as the high

A promotional picture of the early seventies, using light and shadow to hide the effect of Bell's Palsy. (Photo by David Street, courtesy of Lightfoot)

point in Lightfoot's yearly schedule. The Riverboat eventually struggled to an end in the late seventies, (it is now the trendy brick home in Yorkville to a hairdresser and two expensive boutiques), a victim to its small size, the rising salary demands of the best acts, and the lowering of the drinking age in Ontario to nineteen. A new generation of teenagers was unwilling to patronize places where alcohol was not served, and coffeehouses across the province died for lack of business.

Bernie Fiedler, whom Lightfoot describes as "an old crony," had begun producing the Massey Hall concerts in 1968 and had continued ever since. He still does, to this day. The concerts had now grown to a series of five, totalling over thirteen thousand paid admissions each year. The people of Toronto and Lightfoot had continued their unique performer-audience relationship (which still survives today, with many of the same people who attended in the sixties now bringing along their sons and daughters).

In December of 1973, the marriage of Lightfoot and Brita was officially ended. Upon returning from a European holiday, Brita had found "another woman" sharing her matrimonial bed. Lightfoot denies that there ever was any such woman, but Brita asserts that she had proof of a woman in her house, a woman who worked in the basement of Sunnybrook Hospital. By now, it really doesn't matter anymore. The marriage then only a game of self-delusion on both sides, she sued for divorce. By the terms of the divorce, Brita received the largest settlement in Canadian legal history, a record held until that time by the wife of hockey star Bobby Hull. Brita retained custody of the two children, which was no doubt for the best, considering Lightfoot's tumultuous living habits. The presiding judge, Mr. Justice Frank Donnelly, awarded her a cash settlement of $150,000 and a $4,500 per month maintenance allowance, estimating it would take a net income of $30,000 a year for Brita to live in the style to which she had become accustomed. Later, Lightfoot deeded the Blythwood house to her, in lieu of the lump sum cash settlement. Accepting that deal was a smart move by Brita, for the value of the house skyrocketed in the wild Toronto real estate market and when she sold it recently the proceeds made her what Lightfoot calls "a wealthy woman."

It is said that her lawyer, Harvey Bliss, at the end of the trial, added insult to Lightfoot's injury by crooning "That's what you get for lovin' me..." as he left the courtroom.

Brita later returned to Europe for two years with the children, in order to give them a European education. When she returned to Canada she settled back into the house on Blythwood (recently torn down to make way for a row of expensive townhouses). She now lives in Unionville, Ontario and today she is bitter that she did not fight for an even larger divorce settlement. This bitterness does not make her any different from a million other wives who do not share in their ex-husbands' ultimate wealth which, after all, they helped to create in earlier and happier days.

To those who might criticize Brita's attitude, it must be pointed out that when she met Lightfoot and married him he did not have a lot of money, only hopes and expectations, and that life inside her marriage in that basement apartment on Arlington Avenue was as hellish as any bad marriage anywhere. If there is bitterness, perhaps it is deserved.

Early the next year, Lightfoot's new album *Sundown*, and the single of the same title both went to Number One on the American record charts. Finally, after all the struggle and turmoil and work and sweat, Lightfoot had the reward all musicians want and value, the reward that all pop musicians crave and need: he had his Number One Gold Single. Finally, he had the tangible proof that he had made it in the

States, right along with Elvis and Dylan and the Beatles and the Stones.

Quietly but effectively Lightfoot was solidifying his reputation and appeal in the United States. He received the best reviews of his career when the New York *Times* described a concert at Philharmonic Hall as being "as austere as a Samuel Beckett play." Clearly, his marital difficulties, his drinking problem and his ill health were all contributing to a public persona which was strangely appealing, perhaps because the lyrics and the melodies of his songs were clearly romantic, while the singer himself remained cool and aloof.

Cathy Smith was happier during this period, for she saw a way of ending her relationship with Lightfoot. Behind Lightfoot's back, the producer of the *Sundown* album, Leonard Waronker ("Lenny" to his friends) hired her to do some background vocals on the title song. When it became a hit, she achieved some stature in the recording industry. She immediately sought employment as a singer with Murray McLauchlan, by this time himself a successful Toronto folksinger who, while not as popular as Lightfoot, had his own devoted following.

Lightfoot was enraged by her act which he felt to be a crass betrayal. To him, McLauchlan, friend though he might be, was still "the competition." Working for him was an act of betrayal far worse than a sexual infidelity. The resulting screaming argument marked the real end of their relationship, although it somehow stumbled along in simmering anger and in bitter recrimination for two more years.

Lightfoot's medication for the Bell's Palsy, together with his ever-increasing alcohol consumption, increased his moodiness and surliness. He became increasingly critical of the musicians he worked with, and fired and hired them, seemingly at will. He became obsessed with musical perfection and began to take bizarre steps to achieve a musical purity in his guitar playing. In truth, his audience couldn't have cared less about his guitar playing. He was perceived as a singer and songwriter, not as a master guitarist like Eric Clapton or Jimmy Page. But nobody dared mention that to Lightfoot.

He began wearing a glove on his left hand at all times, even in the shower, to protect the calluses on his picking hand. He refused to allow a live performance recording to be released because he thought he heard a flaw in the guitar playing caused by a broken fingernail. Although nobody else could hear the supposedly scratchy sound (he wore a false fingernail), Lightfoot preferred to throw away the twenty thousand dollars the record cost than to release the recording.

Because he still had not recovered the full use of the muscles on one side of his face, all photographs of him were taken to hide the lop-sided look apparent when looking at him straight-on. Lightfoot had, since the beginning of his career, been acutely aware of, and actively involved in, the necessity to create and nurture a public persona that was attractive and comfortable for him, a persona that, if not exactly true, was easy to play and attractive to the public. While he was embarrassed by the flaw in his appearance, he had by now had enough experience in image-moulding to go along with the photographic tricks which implied that nothing really had changed, that this was still the same old Lightfoot in that publicity photo, on that album cover. His audience was no more aware of his disease than it was of the more sordid details of his personal life.

He was not happy with his vocals on *Sundown* and stayed away from the recording studio for over a year. He became ever more reclusive, venturing from his Rosedale mansion to perform concerts in America and Europe, enjoying another hit single from the album, the song "Carefree

With Gordon, Sr., in Orillia shortly before his death.

Cathy Smith cooking dinner for Lightfoot in happier times.

Highway." But, for the first time in his career, he was
starting to get bad reviews for his casual attitude in his
concerts and for what was perceived as the deteriorating
quality of his songwriting. Most critics hated "Carefree
Highway." And yet, he was drawing bigger crowds than
ever before. For the first time, the line was being drawn
between those who loved Lightfoot's music and those who,
like a reviewer for *Rolling Stone* magazine, found his image
as "a middle-aged, wired up folkie in cowboy drag" to be
obscene. But, by the mid-seventies, Lightfoot had struck
such a resonant chord with his audience that bad reviews,
sloppy concerts, failed singles, bad health, imperfect songwriting, careless singing, nothing could lessen the affection
in which he was held.

The death of his father in March 1974 was another
emotional blow in a year filled with inner turmoil. Lightfoot, Sr., had died of cancer in Orillia's Soldier's Memorial
Hospital at the age of sixty-three. Lightfoot had seen his
father the day before he died. Now he was gone.

Lightfoot took his medication, drank his booze and
worried about his guitar technique.

Chapter 8

Hurtin' Songs

In 1975, Lightfoot was thirty-six years old. He had been a major pop star in Canada for a decade, and in the United States for a third of that time. He was many times a millionaire and now lived in the style his vast fortune could command. That year, he made yet another move, to the house which he still owns, a century-old Victorian mansion on Beaumont Road in the exclusive Rosedale section of Toronto. Rosedale is a twisted maze of treed streets and avenues between the Don Valley and Yonge Street north of Bloor. It is usually described as an "old money" neighbour-hood, home to Toronto's elite children and grandchildren of the buccaneers and robber barons who amassed the original fortunes by which these towered red-brick man-sions could be acquired or built. In Montreal the equivalent neighbourhood is Westmount, in Ottawa it is Rockcliffe and in Vancouver, Shaughnessy. Lightfoot's neighbours are very wealthy and very discreet and include the Basset family and Emmett Cardinal Carter. Many of them winter in southern condos, and in the summer take their families up Highway 11, past Orillia and the Gordon Lightfoot sign to the luxurious rusticity of the Muskokas.

Lightfoot's mansion is similar to and completely different

from those of his neighbours. Similar in its Victorian architecture, its manicured lawns, the spaciousness of its massive high-vaulted rooms. Different in the centrepiece of the living room—a massive Steinway grand piano in front of a broad bay window; a Tiffany lamp hung over the pool table which defines what might in a less elegant home be referred to as the "rec room;" the various awards and mementoes that mark the owner's musical career: Markle paintings, a detailed model of the Great Lakes freighter, the Edmund Fitzgerald, on display, statues and drawings of Don Quixote (a character to whom Lightfoot has always felt drawn and about whom he has sung), the collection of wine bottles on the window sill of a spacious sunroom.

In 1975, his financial affairs were well in order, but other parts of his life were not in such good shape.

Cathy and he had finally, irrevocably, angrily broken up for the last time, Cathy heading for California to work as a back-up singer with country pop-singer Tom Paxton, Lightfoot heading into the studio to make a new record tentatively titled *Rainy Day People*. The title song of that album was a description of his relationship with Cathy, a song of tenderness, loneliness and regret, a song built upon the chords of alternating sweetness and bitterness. In perhaps what is the ultimate triumph of the artist over his material, the seven-year-long on-and-off relationship was, in the end, summed up exquisitely in the two minutes and twenty-eight seconds of a hit single.

Eventually, Lightfoot changed the album's title to *Cold on the Shoulder*. It was not well-received critically and did not sell well, except for the single "Rainy Day People." Musically, Lightfoot was beginning a descent into safeness and sameness.

Cold on the Shoulder did hold one or two musical surprises, such as the five-minute tale of racial discrimination leading to death on an Indian reservation in 1910, called "Cherokee Bend." And, somewhere amid the folk and country songs like "Bend in the Water" and "Cold on the Shoulder," there is the unmistakable echo of St. Paul's United Church in Orillia in Lightfoot's gospel-tinged piano-playing on the song "Bells of the Evening," which might be Lightfoot's attempt at a secular hymn for the seventies.

For his next album, rather than try to create new material, Lightfoot continued his battle against United Artists. In Toronto's Eastern Sound Studio, just down the street from the Riverboat in Yorkville, he re-recorded all of his best early material, including "I'm Not Sayin'," "Ribbon of Darkness," "Canadian Railroad Trilogy," "Early Morning Rain," and eight others. He included this material with all of his Warner Brothers hits and released a two-record set called *Gord's Gold*. He was determined to have the last laugh on United Artists. The release of this greatest hits package marked another year of lackadaisical effort.

At the end of the year, however, his spirit was lifted and his determination renewed when Bob Dylan came into town. In one of his many reincarnations as a master of pop self-renewal, Dylan had spent most of 1975 touring the small clubs and halls of America with a motley crew of musical friends he called the Rolling Thunder Review (named, in an ironic twist, after the Pentagon's code name for the saturation bombing techniques used by the American military in North Vietnam). His musical friends included Joan Baez, Joni Mitchell, Roger McGuinn, Ramblin' Jack Elliot, and an assortment of other musicians who were invited to join in at various points on the tour. Playwright Sam Shepard was on the tour as resident scribe.

When the Rolling Thunder Review rolled into Toronto in December 1975, Lightfoot and Ronnie Hawkins joined in for the two shows at Maple Leaf Gardens. Lightfoot had been invited to the musical event of the year, and was clearly touched by Dylan's invitation—Dylan who had remained one of his musical heroes.

At the piano in the Beaumont Road house. (Photo by
Tom Bert, courtesy of Lightfoot)

With Dylan at Mariposa on Centre Island. (Photo by Bruce Cole, courtesy
of Lightfoot)

Lightfoot threw a huge party in the Beaumont Road house. True to form, he and Dylan crept away to an upstairs bedroom to trade songs. Lightfoot sang Dylan's "Ballad in Plain D" into a small tape recorder which Dylan had taken to carrying everywhere. Later, Dylan would use the recording on the soundtrack of his disastrous movie *Renaldo and Clara*.

The meaning of the Rolling Thunder Review was largely in the sense of extended family that Dylan tried to create on the tour, which included all the friends, wives, lovers and children who cared to come along on his crazy odyssey across North America. The Rolling Thunder Review was clearly not touring the way Lightfoot and most musicians knew. But the atmosphere of musical family must have been striking to all those who, even if only for a short time, joined in.

The experience of working with Dylan clearly revived Lightfoot, for he quickly cleared his head and made a host of decisions for the future. His recording contract was coming to an end, and he began formulating plans to renew himself musically in 1976. He wrote dozens of new songs, saving the best ones for his next album.

But first, he would make some business moves.

In a move to consolidate his business affairs even more in his own hands, he fired Al Mair from Early Morning Productions, and hired his older sister, Beverley Lightfoot Eyers, as his business manager. Mair, along with Tom Williams, a former publicist, had formed Attic Records, which eventually became a successful independent Canadian label. The reason for the split between Lightfoot and Mair, according to the latter, was that "Gordon could not handle the competition of one of his people promoting other acts."

Lightfoot is hurt by this allegation, pointing out that Mair had worked on the formation of Attic Records for at least a year before Lightfoot got upset. Talking to Lightfoot today, it becomes clear that this incident reflects, for him, the meaning of loyalty. Mair, like others before and after him, lacked the depth of loyalty required by the stern Lightfoot. Loyalty cuts two ways, however. Try to get Lightfoot to go further than setting the record straight, try to goad him into maligning a person from his past; you will see that it cannot be done.

He does not forgive, but he does not air his grievances publicly, either. Nor does he forget; no, not for Lightfoot the calm of sleep easing the pains of old memories; old memories are never far from the surface of his mind, ready to burst into song lyric as gentle reminiscence or surprisingly bitter barb. Memories are the source of his muse and the bread of daily life. Asked about a remark attributed to Mair, his head turns sharply, his eyes flash as he asks, "You got that from *Maclean's* magazine, didn't you?" referring to an article written more than a decade ago. He might not know every word of that long-ago article, but you can bet your mortgage money he knows the gist of it. Forget not, lest you be condemned to repeating your mistakes.

Hiring Bev was a shrewd move, for she guided Lightfoot's business with a sure hand for the next eight years, increasing his fortune to unprecedented levels. She had two major assets to bring to the role of manager: as a family member, she was completely trustworthy (and Lightfoot had, for some years, been exhibiting increasing paranoia about business), and she loved Lightfoot enough to tell him the truth when she felt he was in the wrong, especially in his personal life. And, God knows, he needed some help in re-shaping his personal life during those days at the end of the seventies.

It was Lightfoot's father who had first suggested that he hire Bev. "I hadn't thought of it, but when Dad made the suggestion, I realized it was a great idea," he says. And it worked. "Apart from the great work she did in the business, she was instrumental in getting me to stop drinking."

A romantic story abounds that Lightfoot made a deathbed promise to his father to hire Bev. It is a story too mythical to be true, and Lightfoot recalls that his father made the suggestion long before his death.

Shortly after Bev joined Early Morning Productions, negotiations were concluded with Warner Brothers for a new recording contract. Once again, it was one of the most lucrative in the business. The relationship between Lightfoot and Warners was a happy one, both sides extremely pleased at his new-found recording success in America.

Stung by the bad reviews of his album, *Cold on the Shoulder*, Lightfoot hurled himself into the writing and recording of a new record, *Summertime Dream*. He was determined to make it his best work yet, filling it with the finest material he had written in years. For his efforts, he got a new hit single and a hit album. The album *Summertime Dream* sold one hundred thousand copies in Canada in its first week, and went on to become Lightfoot's bestselling album in the United States. Once more, he was on top of his game, ready to take on all comers.

His new hit single was perhaps the strangest hit in the history of recorded music. At more than six minutes in length, it was not a song of romance and sex, but rather a song about a shipwreck. It was called "The Wreck of the Edmund Fitzgerald."

Lightfoot had gotten the idea for the song by reading an article in *Newsweek* detailing the shipwreck on Lake Superior of the iron ore carrier the Edmund Fitzgerald, which sank in a gale with all twenty-nine men on board, in November 1975. The story of the shipwreck was terrifying, a story of the small heroisms of life and the tragedies of sudden death.

Jessie and Bev Lightfoot, backstage at Massey Hall. (Photo by David Street, courtesy of Lightfoot)

Lightfoot's band, backstage at Massey Hall (Terry Clements, Mike Heffernan, Barry Keane, Lightfoot, Pee Wee Charles, Rick Haynes). (Photo by David Street, courtesy of Lightfoot)

Lightfoot felt compelled to write what he called "a memorial" to the crew of the ship. As he had once before, with "The Canadian Railroad Trilogy," Lightfoot found, in "The Wreck of the Edmund Fitzgerald," a subject for a song which resonated within the unconscious of the nation, a story which millions of Canadians and Americans found so compelling that listening to the song on the radio became almost an act of self-hypnotism. Listening to the song, even today, is like listening to a national anthem or a favourite childhood hymn, an experience so foreign to the normal act of listening to pop music that whenever it is heard sur-rounded by the jingles and rock music of commercial radio it seems to make everything still and silent, it seems to compel all listeners to pause and to stop all activity and to listen, just listen, to the sweet and sad elegy of twenty-nine sailors dead beneath the cold waters of Lake Superior.

"The Wreck of the Edmund Fitzgerald" is so foreign to all the sensibilities of popular music in the second half of the twentieth century that it does not deserve the status of being referred to only as a hit record; it is more in the nature of being a religious experience akin to attending a funeral. Although Lightfoot would continue to find striking themes and resonant images in his work over the next decade (in "East of Midnight" and "Ghosts of Cape Horn," for example), the coming together of the Death March-like music and the lyric intensity of the story-telling in "Wreck" stands as the high point in his creative efforts.

Lightfoot had, himself, been sailing on Lake Superior, and knew what it was like to confront its viciousness when winds were at gale-force. He owned his own sailing vessel and confided to friends and interviewers that he planned to take the government navigation course which would permit him to become a master of a Great Lakes sailing vessel. Like many other Orillia natives reared within walking distance of the harbourfront, he had fallen prey to the mystique of water travel. Canoeing and sailing became his recreation and his refuge. Vic Carpenter, a master-builder of sailing ships in Port McNichol at the south end of Georgian Bay, built him a sleek forty-five-foot mahogany sloop. The boat, which sleeps six in comfort, was christened "The Golden Goose." Lightfoot sailed it for a half-decade and, although he eventually sold it when finding time in which to sail became a problem, the "Goose" is still remembered by the locals for its beauty. Even now, Lightfoot sails every year with Vic in Carpenter's own mahogany sloop, the "Coffee Grinder," an exact replica of "The Golden Goose."

From the proceeds of a Lightfoot benefit concert in Traverse City, Michigan, a scholarship fund of eleven thousand dollars, in memory of two naval cadets who had died in the Edmund Fitzgerald sinking, was set up to benefit future cadets at the Great Lakes Maritime Academy. Although ideas for several movies based on his song were bandied about by producers, Lightfoot resisted efforts to over-expoit the tragedy, accepting the guidance of a group of wives of the deceased sailors, with whom he kept in touch for many years.

Lightfoot plunged into the recording of a new album, called *Endless Wire*, in August 1976. The proceedings were stormy and continued what was to become yet another repetitive pattern, that of throwing away expensive tapes and re-recording material until he was totally satisfied.

The year 1976 was to be Lightfoot's benefit concert year. In April he had organized a benefit for the Canadian Track and Field Association and the Canadian Olympic Association. The Olympics were being held in Montreal that year and Lightfoot had read an article detailing the financial plight of the Canadian athletes. Hoping to raise two hundred thousand dollars, he contacted Sylvia Tyson, classical guitarist Liona Boyd, and Murray McLauchlan, all of whom agreed to appear for free. Concert-goers thought McLauchlan stole the show.

Although the concert, held at Maple Leaf Gardens (home of the Toronto Maple Leafs hockey team, of which Lightfoot was an avid fan) was sold out, the proceeds fell short of the projected gate. Lightfoot threw an extra ten thousand dollars of his own money into the kitty, and convinced one of the sponsors, Carling O'Keefe Breweries (who had already donated one hundred thousand dollars to cover the cost of a CBC televised version of the concert) to match his donation, in order to make the two-hundred-thousand-dollar figure which had been promised.

There were those who suggested that the benefit was a public relations gesture on Lightfoot's part to endear himself further to the Canadian public, and to latch onto the Olympics bandwagon of that year. Countering such criticism, Lightfoot referred to his own athletic prowess, no doubt exaggerated, as a teenager. "When I was in high school I was a pole vaulter and a shot putter. I was senior champion in my high school in Orillia," he boasted to an interviewer. He pointed out that all the acts he had chosen to appear at the benefit were solvent in their own careers, and did not need either money or publicity. But Al Mair, who has remained bitter at Lightfoot ever since his departure from Early Morning Productions, was more cynical. "Gordon Lightfoot will not do anything for nothing, for anyone," he snarled in that 1978 interview with *Maclean's* magazine which Lightfoot still remembers.

The truth of it is that Lightfoot has done several benefits to aid charitable causes, but he picks the events very carefully (in his career he has done only a few benefits in his home town of Orillia) and the positive publicity about each charitable act no doubt helps his public relations. All famous performers are continuously begged for donations

Murray McLauchlan, Liona Boyd, Sylvia Tyson and Lightfoot, at the 1976 Olympic benefit show (Photo by John Rowlands, courtesy of Canada Wide Feature Services Ltd.)

With James Taylor, John Denver and Harry Chapin, backstage at a benefit concert at the Joe Lewis Arena in Detroit in the late seventies.

of time and talent to charities, and Lightfoot has contributed to no less than necessary and no more than expected. In recent years, however, he has increased his commitment to charitable causes, especially world hunger and environmental concerns.

For all pop singers, charitable donations of talent are seen as part of a wider public relations strategy. Whether or not any true feelings exist toward a particular charity, most entertainers make sure that their generosity gains the attention of the media. Lightfoot's own public relations seem erratic at best, but he has maintained his success for so many years that who is to gainsay his efforts? Al Mair suggests that Lightfoot was influenced by Dylan's habit of maintaining an elusive and mysterious image in his public persona, and this has been the reason for Lightfoot's reluctance to sit still for extended interviews and regular appearances on television. Lightfoot perhaps said it best when he noted that he hated interviews because whatever answer he gave to a question made him "look stupid."

When you're heading into your forties, the years seem to start slipping by, each one going faster and faster than the last until a year, a decade, a life has irretrievably disappeared. For Lightfoot, the years since 1976 seem to have gone by faster than most. In those days he appeared to be in the full stride of mid-career, but today the mid-seventies stand revealed as the apex of his creative achievements. If he once spoke to us about all our innermost desires and lusts, he now seems irrelevant, a man who still writes and sings about all the same things he always did, but a man to whom nobody is listening anymore. There is a sadness about that. Perhaps we don't listen anymore not because what he is saying is intrinsically unimportant, but because we've heard it all too often and hearing about it one more time does not seem to lead us any more into doing something about it. We all still fumble around in our love affairs, we all still hurt each other, we all still ignore each other when we need each other the most, we all still say the most cruel and unnecessary things and walk away from each other and slam the doors of indifference behind us. That's not Lightfoot's fault. Even if we don't listen anymore, he's still out there producing albums and writing love songs and coming to your home town for one more concert.

But, after the year of 1976, the hit records wouldn't come anymore, the critics who once were almost idolatrous in their adulation began saying unkind things about his music, and his audience which had once so loved him now treated him with cool indifference.

Lightfoot never seemed to care. He just kept on working hard, withdrawing into an ever-decreasing circle of friends, and using his vast fortune as a buffer against decline.

And, true to habit of repetition, Lightfoot once more moved into a troubled relationship with yet another woman, a relationship that, like all others, would ultimately degenerate into recrimination and separation.

The woman was another Cathy: Cathy Coonley, a friendly, attractive tall blonde from Miami, Florida. In 1975, she moved into Lightfoot's Rosedale mansion in a spirit of love and optimism. Like Brita and like the "other" Cathy, she too would run from the excesses of Lightfoot's behaviour. But, for the moment, romance obscured all defects.

Cathy Coonley had met Lightfoot in Florida, where she was attending one of his concerts and trying to photograph him. Seeing that the security guards were bothering her, Bernie Fiedler came to her rescue and, taken with her charm and openness, introduced her to Lightfoot. Lightfoot was also taken with Coonley but was already committed for the evening so he asked her out another time. They got along well, and Lightfoot invited her to look him up the next time she was in Toronto.

She was in Toronto in June, and called Fiedler, who

passed on the message. Lightfoot called her in the midnight hours. "What are you doing? Get over here." She went.

When she arrived, Lightfoot was in the process of moving from his Bin-Scarth Road home to his Beaumont Road mansion. Coonley pitched in and helped him move his things. Symbolically, this move must have been a purging of Cathy Smith from his past.

Coonley was in Toronto to meet friends who were going on a sailing trip. The trip ended in the Azores, with Coonley flat broke. She called Lightfoot to tell him of her predicament. He wired her money for her air fare back to Toronto.

They began an affair, and by September she had moved in with him. The love affair was, once more, to last seven years.

By now Lightfoot was remorseful about the violence that had plagued his relationship with Cathy Smith. He treated Cathy Coonley with infinitely more gentleness. "There was never any physical violence," Cathy insists about the seven years that they lived together. "At times there was yelling and screaming...but that was on both sides." Both admit to "a little" violence that did not continue, partly because Lightfoot was genuine in his sorrow about his past, and partly because Coonley was ready to give as good as she got.

After his *Endless Wire* album, Lightfoot fell into a fallow period, finding it difficult to write new material. He poured himself into his new love affair, sailed and canoed, listened to other people's music and withdrew still further from public view. He had no financial worries: by this time, his annual income from royalties exceeded a half-million dollars each year (over one hundred singers had recorded "If You Could Read My Mind" alone). Income from recordings and a somewhat less hectic concert pace of touring combined to more than double that figure. He was doing not too badly. Whatever demons that might have tortured him were being held at bay with copious amounts of alcohol.

And Cathy, who had not been much of a drinker, was starting to join him in his partying, drinking champagne on more than just joyous occasions.

But all those years of partying, quaffing that ale, sipping that wine, shooting down the whiskey, the years of bitterness and violence and regret, all those years of keeping his habits secret from his public were to be revealed. The toll taken by those years would some day have to be accounted for and redeemed.

At 2:18 A.M. on February 16, 1978, Lightfoot's Cadillac was stopped by the police as he was driving on Dixon Road near Highway 27 in the Toronto suburb of Etobicoke, near Toronto's Lester Pearson International Airport. His heavy drinking was about to be made public for the first time.

Lightfoot was driving with his high beams on, and police officer Timothy Hill stopped him and invited him to take a breathalyzer test on the portable ALERT unit he had in his cruiser. The machine's reading was 110 milligrams of alcohol per 100 millilitres of blood. The legal limit in Ontario is 80 milligrams. Lightfoot was asked to accompany the officer to the station. There, he was tested on an official breathalyzer machine, and he registered an even higher reading, 120 milligrams, 50 percent over the limit. He was released and driven home while the machinery of legal prosecution moved against him.

On February 19, he was officially charged with impaired driving. The trial date was set for August 16. Lightfoot hired Toronto lawyer Gerald Kluwak to defend him.

The trial, before Provincial Judge Sydney M. Roebuck, lasted only forty-five minutes. Deputy Crown Attorney Norman Matusiak first called Constable Hill to testify about the circumstances by which Lightfoot's car was stopped and to give evidence of the results of the first breathalyzer. Then, he called Constable Roman Guglielmi to testify about the reading of the second test. Kluwak called no witnesses.

Judge Roebuck was still apparently unsatisfied that the

With Cathy Coonley.

The "Golden Goose."

breathalyzer results clearly indicated Lightfoot's alcohol level at the time he was driving, and asked the prosecutor how he planned to prove the point.

Matusiak, feeling that the point had been well-proved already, replied, "It's a logical and natural inference, Your Honour."

His Honour disagreed. He said that the Crown's case was all conjecture, and added, "Based on the evidence I have heard there is nothing relating the readings to the amount of alcohol he had at the time he was stopped. Based on the evidence, this court dismisses the charge."

While Lightfoot was understandably elated, Matusiak was stunned. Speaking to reporters after the trial, he stormed that "the implications of this case are such that I am obliged to consider an appeal." He indicated that all similar cases awaiting trial could be adjourned until an appeal court made a ruling. He immediately sought, and received, permission to appeal.

The appeals were to be heard right up to the Supreme Court of Canada over the next three years. While it must have seemed important to Lightfoot to try to clear himself of the charges, the last thing he needed was public discussion over a three-year period of his drunk driving. In retrospect, he might have been wiser to pay his fine and let the matter rest.

Perhaps Lightfoot has a secret fondness for the law, perhaps in another life he would have made a wonderful trial lawyer. Whatever the reason—and it may only be the vast reservoir of stubbornness and sensitivity to criticism he has deep inside—he seems to revel in the intricacies of legal manoeuvering, even if he always seems, in the end, to lose.

His long, protracted battle over a simple charge of impaired driving, it would seem, could serve no useful purpose for his public relations even if he somehow managed to beat the charge on a technicality.

But fight he would. And lose he would.

Chapter 9

East of Midnight

For the moment, having won acquittal, he continued his concert touring, avoiding the recording studio. By the late seventies, touring meant hopping on a chartered Lear 35 jet to take him across North America. Despite the lyrics of his first famous song, Lightfoot could indeed now hop a jet plane as easily as earlier generations once hopped freight trains.

One advantage of his lowered public profile was that he could stroll the streets of Toronto unrecognized and not bothered by his fans. Despite the years in the public eye, it nevertheless seemed that his public still did not have a good idea of exactly how Lightfoot looked in person.

On May 3, 1979, Mr. Justice Sydney Robins of the Ontario Supreme Court heard the Crown's appeal against Lightfoot's acquittal. The appeal turned on a point of law concerning whether oral testimony by a police officer, rather than a written certificate of analysis of the results of a breathalyzer test, was enough evidence to convict a person. Crown Attorney Matusiak argued that he had not introduced such a certificate into evidence because he thought that the sworn testimony of an officer was legally more effective.

Mr. Justice Robins agreed with Matusiak and, considering four different highly technical questions of law, decided that Judge Roebuck had erred in not accepting the oral evidence of the officer and the result of the breathalyzer instrument. He overturned the acquittal. This time, it was Lightfoot who filed for leave to appeal.

At the end of the year, Lightfoot finally re-entered Eastern Sound Studio to record his next album, *Dream Street Rose*, released early in 1980. Perhaps everyone had heard it all once too often. Once again, he didn't have a hit single, and the record made only the very bottom position on the charts.

Lightfoot was seemingly unconcerned. For the moment, he had a new interest: he wanted to act in movies. Levon Helm and, later, Robbie Robertson of The Band were both starting new careers in Hollywood. After some twenty years, The Band had finally broken up, with an appropriately named final concert called *The Last Waltz*, lovingly filmed by Martin Scorsese and released as a highly successful documentary. Levon Helm obtained a role in the movie *Coal Miner's Daughter*, the film biography of country singer Loretta Lynn, starring Cissy Spacek, who won an Academy Award for her portrayal. While Levon hadn't won any awards, the critics were highly impressed by his acting debut.

Acting seemed a strange choice of a second career for Lightfoot. He had never been renowned for his verbal skills and despite his many years of concerts and television appearances, still seemed stiff and ill-at-ease in public. Then there was the Bell's Palsy. By 1980, he had recovered most of his facial motor functions, but he never smiled in public. He simply couldn't. Any movie role he got had better be of a dour, unsmiling character.

That character was exactly what he was asked to play in his first film, *Harry Tracy, Desperado*.

Lightfoot's sister, Bev, and his new girlfriend, Cathy, both encouraged Lightfoot to try his hand at films, so he

Lightfoot and his band board the Lear Jet in Salt Lake City, Utah (pilot, co-pilot, Barry Keane, Terry Clements, Pee Wee Charles, Rick Haynes, Mike Heffernan and Lightfoot).

As Marshal Morrie Nathan in Harry Tracy, Desperado.

hired the ICM talent agency in Los Angeles to represent him. Because of his fame in the music industry, he was almost immediately offered a chance to appear in three different films. One was a Burt Reynolds' car-chase film, another a Steve McQueen film which was suspended when McQueen became ill with cancer, and the third was a western starring Bruce Dern. Because Lightfoot admired Dern's work, he chose the western, *Harry Tracy*, and offered to audition.

The producers, Sid and Marty Krofft, sent him a script and he memorized his part. While in Los Angeles playing at the Amphitheatre, he auditioned in the Kroffts' Hollywood offices, where he met Dern. The next day he was offered the part. He still couldn't smile.

Like any novice actor happy at landing his first role, Lightfoot immediately took acting lessons and even riding lessons at Humber College in Toronto to prepare for his part. *Harry Tracy* was an American-Canadian co-production, and there may be some truth in rumours that Lightfoot actually got the part to help the production fulfil the Canadian content rules imposed by one of the film's financial backers, the Canadian Film Development Corporation. The rumours didn't bother Lightfoot.

The film had some heavyweight actors. In addition to Dern, who played the desperado of the title, actress Helen Shaver (also a Canadian) played Dern's girlfriend. The novices included Lightfoot, who played the part of Marshal Morrie Nathan, a historical character who spent most of the movie trying to catch Harry Tracy, and Cathy Coonley, who had a bit part as a prostitute. William Graham, who had previously directed the critically-acclaimed *Guyana Tragedy*, was the director. Producer Ron Cohen of Montreal represented the Canadian money.

Like most films produced to take advantage of tax write-offs and Canadian content regulations, *Harry Tracy*,

Desperado, failed miserably on every level. The film got bad reviews. Bruce Dern got bad reviews. Helen Shaver got bad reviews. Gordon Lightfoot got bad reviews, although he escaped relatively unscathed since not a lot had been expected of him. Worse than the reviews was the fact that the film lost a lost of money (it had been budgeted at eight-and-a-half million dollars) and was quickly pulled from the theatres, to appear occasionally on late night television, the graveyard of failed movies. Lightfoot's film career was over, for the moment.

In May of 1981, the Supreme Court of Canada finally heard Lightfoot's appeal on his impaired driving conviction. The Court ruled against Lightfoot, referring the case back to the original court. Chief Justice Bora Laskin, writing for the court, ruled that Judge Roebuck had originally erred in not accepting the oral evidence of the police officers as sufficient proof of guilt, noting that "nothing more is required, in the absence of any evidence to the contrary." Lightfoot would have to face Judge Roebuck once more, this time his guilt assured.

Before his trial date, he toured Ireland and England. A week after the Supreme Court decision, he was in Belfast, playing to an excited crowd of two thousand Catholics and Protestants. Although the concert-goers had put aside their religious differences for the moment, gunshots and an IRA rocket blast from two blocks away could clearly be heard from Grosvenor Hill, site of the concert.

The police frisked everyone entering the hall and patrolled the lobby in flak jackets. Once inside, nobody could leave until the concert was over (if anyone planted a bomb, they, too, would have to die).

Before the show, tension hung in the air. The night before, in Dublin, a mob of Irish Republicans had rioted during Lightfoot's show, smashing windows at the hotel where he and the band were staying.

Why the IRA was angry at Lightfoot is difficult to say. His childhood Protestantism does not seem to have ever been a serious affair, and none of his song lyrics could be interpreted an anti-Catholic or anti-Irish, except by the most perverted mind. Perhaps it was simply that Lightfoot came from Canada, where the hated Queen of England was still our head of state.

Lightfoot had arrived in Ireland at the worst possible moment, when tensions were at one of the highest points in memory. Pope John Paul II had been shot by a terrorist. England had recently imposed a state of siege against the IRA, arresting suspected terrorists without warrant and holding them without right of habeas corpus, even convicting them without due process of law—all liberties allowed British citizens but denied the Irish. In response, convicted IRA members in prison had gone on a hunger strike. Shortly after Lightfoot arrived for his concert tour, one of the IRA fasters, Francis Hughes, had been allowed by the British to starve himself to death. All of Ireland was a powder keg of hatred and revulsion for the British.

Arriving in Belfast after the show in Dublin, Lightfoot and his band were shocked to find a barbed wire fence surrounding their hotel, and an army guard post at the hotel entrance doing body checks of everyone who entered. It was not only their hotel which was so guarded. At the entrance of every large store in Belfast, body searches were carried out on every shopper. Business streets had checkpoints and armed guards at every corner. British soldiers in battle guard carrying automatic rifles arrogantly strode the streets while army vans with shrieking sirens and flashing blue lights careened through the old cobblestone streets so filled with the history of violence and warfare. Lightfoot had innocently strode into a cauldron of hatred.

In the concert halls of both Belfast and Dublin, however, the audiences forgot the outside world and cheered and applauded Lightfoot as he sang the old songs about true love gone bad, Canadian railroads and Great Lakes shipwrecks. After being informed during the intermission about the Dublin riots, Lightfoot attempted to talk to the audience about what was happening. He was as articulate as anyone could be, faced with such events.

He said, "I don't know what to say. I only wish you all well—and peace." The audience roared its approval of the sentiment and, with the opening lines of his next song, "It doesn't matter if the sun doesn't shine," the hall exploded with applause.

After the Belfast concert, Lightfoot left immediately for Liverpool, Glasgow and London. The British part of the tour did not go as well, probably because Lightfoot had been so shaken by the events in Ireland. He generally received bad press notices, and his final concert in London, at the Dominion Theatre, was an unmitigated disaster. Attempting to speak to the audience, he managed to insult Britain and all Britons. He harangued the audience for half an hour and complained bitterly about the high prices in England. He was clearly nervous and cut the concert short. The audience stormed out angrily, some demanding their money back.

Promoter Andrew Miller pleaded with Lightfoot to return to the stage. Lightfoot finally agreed. Many of the audience members were still in the foyer, so Miller invited them all back inside. Only about twenty of the three hundred audience members returned to hear a few new songs. Defeated, Miller announced that he would refund the money to anyone who asked. With wonderful understatement, he apologized for the shortness of the concert. "The chap was tired," he said.

It is probably no wonder that Lightfoot was tired, and that he was depressed. He was returning to Canada only to once more stand before Judge Roebuck, in the certainty that he would now be convicted of impaired driving.

In early October 1981, he finally was found guilty of driving while intoxicated in 1978. Judge Roebuck fined him all of two hundred dollars. Like some indigent in any of the courts in any of the judicial districts of Canada, Lightfoot asked for thirty days to pay the fine. He was granted his thirty days. His long battle against the legal system was over.

Lightfoot, for the first time in eighteen months, went back into the recording studios to work on a new album. He had a handful of new songs, even if it sometimes seemed now that making a new record was more of a duty than a love.

On December 30, 1981, Cathy Coonley gave birth to a nine-pound baby boy. The understandably proud parents called him Eric. Lightfoot and Coonley's live-in relationship was consistent with the pattern of his previous battles with Brita and Cathy Smith. It was sometimes warm and loving and sometimes filled with yelling and arguing and accusations and recriminations. Lightfoot was still drinking heavily and, although he was not overly violent with her, there can be no doubt that, after the birth of their child, Coonley would have to think hard about raising her son in such a bitter atmosphere.

Shortly after Eric's birth, Lightfoot released his new album, called *Shadows*. The moderate sales of the record were becoming another recurrent pattern. Part of the reason Lightfoot's albums since *Summertime Dream* had not sold terribly well and sounded too similar to each other had to do with his drinking. Despite the painstaking work that went into each record and despite a number of good songs appearing on each album, there seemed to be a lack of creative spark, an absence of energy which was apparent even to his loving public.

His next album, *Salute*, would also follow this pattern. It would not be until his *East of Midnight* album in 1986 that he

With Jessie, Bev and Cathy Coonley at Eric's christening.

Cathy and Eric.

could rightly claim a full return of his creative energies. Today, he ruefully admits, "During the late seventies and early eighties, my records weren't very good."

And yet, if the albums cannot stand as masterpieces, there were a number of individual songs which will continue to be part of our collective memory for a generation: songs like "Ghosts of Cape Horn" and "Alberta Bound," "Shadows," and "Baby, Step Back."

With record sales dwindling, Lightfoot once more stepped up his concert touring to keep in touch with his fans. A sample of his 1982 touring schedule illustrates the pace he was now setting. Between June 18 and October 17, 1982, he performed thirty-one concerts in Canada and the United States, probably grossing over three-quarters of a million dollars for his efforts. During this period, he still managed to take the month of July off as a holiday, to make another canoeing trip to the north. His concert schedule began from Philadelphia and included, among other cities, New York, Cincinnati, Fort Wayne, Saratoga Springs, Los Angeles, Toronto, Reno (for a week at Harrah's Club), Duluth and Minneapolis. Such a schedule would drain the energy of a man half his age. But, there has probably never been a performer so dedicated to his career as Lightfoot. The demands of the road would kill many pop singers through the sixties and seventies and even into the eighties, but Lightfoot is, if anything, a survivor. His attitude seemed to be that if his record sales weren't what they once were he would simply redouble his efforts to play concerts wherever anyone would book him.

Many performers use the concert tour to fill the gaps between hit records (and the gaps sometimes stretch into decades). Lightfoot was following an honoured tradition, but he still wasn't giving up hope for that new hit, which was always going to be just around the corner. Even without another hit record, he was still playing to packed houses everywhere he went.

One of Lightfoot's favourite portraits of himself. (By Jeri L. Rodgers, 1978, courtesy of Lightfoot)

Shortly before he quit drinking in 1982. (Photo courtesy of the Toronto *Star*)

Towards the end of the tour, in mid-September, he arrived at Roy Thompson Hall in Toronto, directly from the South Shore Music Circus in Cohasset, Massachusetts. His mother, Jessie, his girlfriend, Cathy, and his older children, Fred and Ingrid, were all in the audience. He performed what was becoming a standard show, one that would be as pleasing to the audience in North Tonawanda, New York as it was to concert-goers in Concord, California.

By now, he knew it would please them in Toronto, Ontario as well. He had the whole game figured out. They'd never catch him now. He knew what the audience wanted even before they asked for it, even before the audience itself realized what they wanted. At Roy Thompson Hall, when the audience members shouted requests, he cynically gave the show over to them, saying, "It's up to you. You're paying the bread." He sang the songs they requested.

All performers end up in a battle with their audience. Except in the avant-garde, the audience never wants to go where the performer wants to lead it. Often, the audience wants to give its adulation, but the performer is too embarrassed, and too filled with the sense of his own unworthiness, to accept adulation. The audience usually wants to bask in the familiar, the warm and comforting sound of the performer whom it has grown to love. The performer wants to innovate, to introduce new things, to reveal all the aspects of creativity. Audiences hate it when performers try to do things like that. Audiences want to hear that Number One hit that they grew up on, that they fell in love to, that they heard on the car radio all that hot summer up at the cottage. The performer hates doing that song: he sang it last night, and the night before, and a thousand nights before that. They want to hear that song, and they want to hear it right now. And they don't want the performer making fun of that song. They just don't get the joke.

Like a million other performers before him, Lightfoot was on tenterhooks trying to tread the fine line between the joke and the audience's nostalgia for that hot summer up at the cottage. He was succeeding better than most. But it surely was sounding the same every time. And the sameness can drain the soul of an artist.

Perhaps it was just that Lightfoot had already done it all, and there was really nothing left to do.

In the United States, MTV was starting to show music videos twenty-four hours a day instead of regular programming. The new stars were being made on the strength of their visual appearance on video, rather than on the sound of their records. In 1983, Lightfoot made his first music video, perhaps to keep his hand in at acting. Video was a better medium for him, since it was so stylized and he needn't act, really, just lip-sync his songs and wander around in various costumes. Lightfoot's videos are really not very good, especially compared with the innovative work done by singers like Cyndi Lauper and Bruce Springsteen and groups like the Kinks and U2. Once again he would make another annual affair of releasing a single accompanied by a music video.

During 1982, Cathy Coonley had come to a decision. She had to leave Lightfoot. Despite the birth of Eric, the fighting and yelling and screaming had continued, fuelled by the alcohol Lightfoot was consuming. She could not raise a child in that atmosphere. Love might still exist, but it had been buried beneath the bitterness. The love affair was over.

The loss of Cathy and his conviction on the impaired drinking charge seemed to have finally driven home to Lightfoot the ravages that alcohol was taking on his life. He resolved to change and, drawing on all the reserves of stubbornness and self-discipline at his command, he did just that: he stopped drinking. He did what no normal person can do, he just quit, cold turkey, just like that, a snap, nothing to it. Only Lightfoot, and other heavy drinkers who have stopped all of a sudden, can know the pain and hurt that went into that decision. But, in the fall of 1982, he had his last drink.

Today, you will find a dozen people who will proudly take the credit for persuading Lightfoot to go on the wagon. Actually, three people were instrumental: his sister Bev, Cathy Coonley and Dr. Jack Burnbaum.

Both Bev and Coonley had frequently hectored Lightfoot to stop (Brita says she gave him the same advice as early as 1968), but this clearly was not enough. The time had to be right. When asked why it was the fall of 1982, he replies simply, "I was ready."

Lightfoot was directed to Dr. Burnbaum, author of the book, *Cry Anger*, by a Warner Brothers' executive, Larry Green, who knew of Burnbaum's success in helping others. The doctor put Lightfoot on tranquilizers (which he took for only one week) and used a combination of trust ("Promise me you won't take a drink between now and our next meeting") and threats ("We could always put you on the drug Antabuse, which makes you physically ill") to help his patient.

Lightfoot had made his decision to stop drinking on the Labour Day weekend. Six weeks later, while on tour in Victoria, B.C., he drank a half bottle of wine. He had fallen off the wagon so soon. His first defeat.

On the plane trip out of Victoria, the stewardess came by with the drinks cart: What do you want—rye, rum, beer, gin, vodka, white wine, red wine? Lightfoot refused the offer, and his defeat had been balanced by a victory. An important victory. Because that last drink in Victoria, in October of 1982, was his last from that day to this. Once more, he had exerted that control of will he had exhibited since childhood.

He went on a health kick and within a year had lost thirty pounds. Everyone congratulated him and told him how great he looked, although there was a new gauntness to him that, at first glance, was almost frightening. Today, his body is firm and his eyes are clear.

He had won another battle, possibly the most important one in his life. Unfortunately, it was already too late to save his relationship with Coonley, who had finally left him, taking Eric with her.

He turned his energy to music. The years were slipping by.

He still played Massey Hall every year. Each year, along with Lightfoot, the audience got older and older.

At the end of 1983, Bev left Early Morning Productions. She was worn out. She was replaced by Barry Harvey, also from Orillia, but thirteen years Lightfoot's junior.

Barry had been working for EMP as a tour organizer since 1981. He had previously worked for Solid Gold Records, then the largest record company in Canada. Bev had called him to ask for suggestions for a tour manager she needed. "Having faith in the ultimate demise" of the company he was working for, he suggested himself. Bev accepted and he came to EMP. Within a couple of years, he found himself as Lightfoot's business manager.

In 1984, Lightfoot heard from Cathy Smith once more.

After leaving Lightfoot, Cathy had drifted into Toronto's demi-monde of after-hours bars and street-corner drug connections. She had split to California and worked as a back-up singer for several groups. She travelled the world. She lived with the Rolling Stones. And she became a heroin addict.

She got caught in a downward spiral of addiction and defeat, finally becoming a pusher to musicians and actors in Los Angeles. One of her customers was comedian John Belushi.

Accepting the Juno Hall of Fame award from Bob Dylan in 1985. (Photo by Plum Studios, courtesy of Gordon Lightfoot)

Belushi had become famous as a crazy, wild comedian on the *Saturday Night Live* television show on NBC. After leaving the show, he starred in the extremely successful film, *Animal House*. His later pictures had not been as successful and he began his own descent into twin addictions, to cocaine and to heroin.

After one night of particularly heavy doping, Belushi begged Cathy to shoot him up with a "speedball," a combination of heroin and cocaine guaranteed to fry the most resilient brain.

He lay down on his bed and never got up again.

Los Angeles police arrested Cathy and charged her with murder. She fled to Toronto and hired a lawyer, Brian Greenspan, to defend her against extradition. One night, Cathy appeared backstage at Massey Hall, destitute and running from the law. She pleaded with Lightfoot for help.

Bev advised him to refuse. The relationship had, after all, been over for almost a decade. This Cathy Smith was not the same one Lightfoot had once loved. This Cathy Smith was a drug addict and an indicted felon. It would look like blackmail if he gave her money now.

Lightfoot didn't see it that way. Thinking it over, he realized "it was the least I could do." When they had split up, Cathy had not asked for any kind of settlement. The concept that a man takes financial care of his family, no matter how estranged, is deeply imbedded in Lightfoot.

Lightfoot paid her legal bills of thirty-five thousand dollars. They had, after all, had a relationship of some seven years and had lived together for three years. There is no doubt that he really had loved Cathy, and that he was filled with remorse over the direction their troubled affair had taken.

The expansiveness of this gesture is typical of Lightfoot. So many of his friends talk about his "incredible generosity." In moments of candour, however, they take quiet note of the demands such generosity places on the recipient. Lightfoot, they say, can be most generous when the mood is upon him, but he can also turn against a friend in a sudden moment of anger at some slight, real or imagined.

Cathy Smith was lucky. She had been remarkably candid about Lightfoot in her "tell-all" autobiography, *Chasing the Dragon*, but Lightfoot nevertheless made her the object of his generosity. He was no doubt glad to see her return to California. She eventually returned there to face the charges, pleaded "no contest" to involuntary manslaughter and was imprisoned. Upon her release, she moved back to Toronto.

Later in the year, he started work on a new record, one that would take him two-and-a-half years to complete. Aware of what was happening with his record sales, but still determined that he could once more get a bestseller, he enlisted the aid of producer David Foster, of Victoria, British Columbia. Foster was a wonder-kid whose every effort seemed to produce another hit. He specialized in hot synthesized musical effects and persistent percussion effects. Foster was terribly up-to-date, terribly trendy and terribly successful. It seemed like a good idea at the time.

In 1986, Lightfoot's album *East of Midnight* was released. It had taken two-and-a-half years and a half-million dollars to produce. It sounded very modern and hip. It didn't sound like Lightfoot at all. Foster had produced only one song on the album, but he seemed to get all the credit in the media. His one effort not a terribly successful one, it is perhaps fitting that, having been given (by whatever circumstances) credit for the modern sound of the album, he should later take blame for its sales figures.

In 1986, the music industry seemed to agree that Lightfoot's best work was long over. They inducted him into the Juno Awards Hall of Fame. Fittingly, the presentation to him was made by his hero, Dylan. Lightfoot was pleased that Dylan had made the gesture.

The Hall of Fame award put Lightfoot into the company of previous inductees Neil Young, Joni Mitchell and Oscar Peterson. The awards committee had been after Lightfoot for years to accept induction, but he had always refused before. He claimed, "I always felt that it had a 'gold watch' kind of feeling to it and that it sort of implied a condition of semi-retirement." The induction of Neil Young, whose career was still in full blossom, seemed to change that perception, and the idea of at least a semi-retirement did not seem so terrible to a man by now in his late forties.

Back home in Orillia, which Lightfoot had left thirty years before, Bob Thompson of the Champlain Golden "K" Club pitched a great idea he had to the City Council. On January 14, 1986, he proposed that the town should erect signs at Orillia's entrances honouring Lightfoot as a favourite son. Thompson had got the idea when he drove through Brantford, Ontario and saw the signs honouring hockey superstar Wayne Gretzky.

City Council agreed it was a good idea. They got the Twin Lakes Secondary School shop students to build two brown and yellow signs, one for each entrance to town. Lightfoot's name was featured more prominently than the town's name.

At first, his mother thought the idea was wonderful. It was a "great honour," she told the Orillia *Packet and Times*, the town's daily newspaper. Later, she would complain that the signs attracted all sorts of riffraff and troublemakers hell-bent on seeking her out in order to contact her son. She complained to the town council, and the original signs were taken down and replaced with more modest ones. At least in Orillia, Lightfoot was still a hero.

Chapter 10

A Minor Ballad

If, at age fifty, Lightfoot looks back on his life, what does he see? Does it finally come down to this crazy, wired up folkie in cowboy drag who now lives in a mansion surrounded by the relics of more honours than most people ever dream of in a lifetime, sitting on more money than most people even imagine earning in a lifetime, surrounded by more emptiness than most people could stand in a lifetime?

Well, not exactly. The crazy wired up folkie isn't so crazy anymore. And he isn't wired up anymore. He's been on the wagon for six years. It was a good decision to make. Maybe all the friends and all the lovers he drove away with his excesses will never return, but he can make new friends now, find new lovers who will never know the difference between the new Lightfoot and the old.

That new Lightfoot is the result of incredible willpower, the power of the will to resist the temptations of the flesh. He has lost the excess poundage that was the inevitable result of all those years of abusive living. The fleshy Lightfoot of his middle years has been replaced by the thin Lightfoot of his late forties, thinness to the point where the

Eric in front of the Beaumont Road house.

Elizabeth Moon on a holiday with Lightfoot in Carmel, California, June 1988.

Lightfoot, Elizabeth Moon, Barry Harvey and Jessie outside Carnegie Hall, New York.

flesh is tight to the bones, a thinness that almost looks alarming, but also bespeaks muscle and sinew.

What about his old friends? All the buddies from his past claim that they're still friends, it's just that they haven't seen him in a decade or more. There's no animosity, everyone says, why he could walk in that door there any minute now and they wouldn't be at all surprised. The only trouble is, he never does walk in that door. Too busy, I guess.

But each year, when Lightfoot appears once more at Massey Hall, some of his old buddies will be in that audience, listening to the old songs and reminiscing about the coffeehouses and taverns of their youth. Now they even bring their kids with them sometimes. Lightfoot sings the old songs and he isn't reminiscing, those songs are still part of the baggage he carries through life, still the main reason he carries on. Maybe the old friends don't see the purpose in doing it anymore, they've all changed careers, they've dropped out somewhere along the road, and Lightfoot is the only one still carrying on.

Family? Bev has left Early Morning Productions, replaced by Barry Harvey. Bev just doesn't give a damn anymore about the music business. There's no family rift. Everyone gets along just fine. But there are hurts and angers that can't be eased even if someone changes their whole life around. Ask anybody, they'll all wonder how Bev could have stood working for her brother for so long.

One of the reasons she could, no doubt, is that she was part of the family effort to help Lightfoot. First it was Jessie, then it was Bev's turn. Bev's son, Stephen is in a band now, and Lightfoot helps that band, too. A family should stick together. Together as much as possible under the circumstances, anyway.

Bev now lives in Barrie, half-way between Orillia and Toronto. When she left Early Morning Productions at the end of 1983, Lightfoot threw a big party for her in his

Rosedale mansion. Almost a hundred people showed up to say goodbye. Lightfoot told the crowd that Bev had "done a superlative job but now wants to do something else with her life." She is doing it in Barrie, back to her small-town roots. Ask Lightfoot about Bev and he will wonder how he would have got along without her. She helped him through a rough period in his life, and now deserves whatever happiness she can find.

And Jessie? She still lives in the family home in Orillia. Lightfoot goes to see her as often as he can. People in town will tell you, why they saw Jessie and Lightfoot have lunch just recently at the Highwayman Inn just outside of town. You might wonder why a millionaire would meet his mother at the Highwayman, rather than in the most posh of restaurants. Probably it's comfortable, it's a reminder of growing up in Orillia. The walls of the Highwayman are covered in pictures of Orillia taken twenty and thirty years ago. There's a town parade, a high school football team, kids playing with their hula hoops, a major fire, and— tucked in with all the rest of the frozen moments of Orillia's past—a photo of Lightfoot and Terry Whelan. They are incredibly young in the picture, the Two-Timers they called themselves then, earnest and dressed-up in a publicity picture taken when all their dreams were young and fresh. Jessie could look at that picture and know she had helped make the two people in the photo; that, without her, none of this would have happened.

Lovers? It's been a long time since Cathy Coonley has gone. Lightfoot has a new love. The new love is Elizabeth Moon. She is a lot younger than he is, but projects quiet assurance in herself and deep affection for him. She met Lightfoot while she was working for Bernie Fieldler. They've been together for about a year now. They seem to be happy. Will this one be the one for all time, the one to erase all the ghosts from the past? Maybe.

Brita's kids have all grown up. Lightfoot didn't really get a chance to see very much of them when they were kids. He missed his first chance at family. Fred has graduated from the University of Toronto and Ingrid is married and has a child, so Lightfoot is a grandfather now. Somehow, looking at him or hearing one of his songs on the radio, it doesn't seem possible that the years have gone by that quickly.

Brita now lives in a big house in a new subdivision in Unionville, just outside of Toronto. Her modern house is filled with heavy, European antiques which project sombreness and stability. It is a house all kids born on the wrong side of the tracks dream of someday owning.

People say that she's still bitter about the divorce and that her only topic of conversation is money. That's not quite true, although when you talk to her you get to understand quickly that financial security is very important to her. "I still wake up fearful that everything is gone," she says. She still feels resentful that Lightfoot was so "irresponsible" as to break up the marriage, resentful especially that Fred grew up without a father's guidance. Brita never did re-marry.

Brita is very careful about what she says concerning Lightfoot. She thinks someday she might write a book about her own life. "My life is far more interesting than his," she smiles. Her comments about her marriage are all allusion and no fact. She hints about being a battered wife, then refuses to amplify. She says there are even worse things in life than violence, then refuses to elaborate. In the end, though, she says simply, "I still love him."

Cathy Coonley's kid, Eric, is now six years old. Lightfoot is making up for his absence as a father during his marriage. He says, "Eric means everything to me." He sees him every week, and pays Cathy a generous child support allowance.

While they were together, Lightfoot and Coonley repeated the pattern of his previous relationships, frequently splitting up, then getting back together again. The turmoil, the ups and downs, the separations, the bickering led Coonley to consider suicide, she says. But there was the other side too, the love and the gentleness and the baby.

Even after the breakup, they tried for several years to somehow make it work again. It just wouldn't, so they have settled for friendship. And the child. And the love it is obvious she still feels for him.

If Lightfoot were to ask you into his living room, he'd probably first have to clear off the toys from the pool table, tidy up the collection of videotapes scattered about and pick up child-things from the floor. He'll tell you what he and Eric did together on the weekend. He'll tell you what a great kid he is, what "a joy" it is to have him around. And Eric is learning that telling people that "Gordon Lightfoot is my dad" will not necessarily keep him out of trouble. It seems like a nice, healthy relationship.

It is a modern fact that fathers nowadays often treat the children of their second family much better than the first kids they had. Lightfoot's absence as a father during his marriage is only normal in these times. We all reap the benefits and pay the price of the modern unshackling of matrimonial bonds. Everyone today seeks dispensation from their marriage vows. Sometimes it's too bad that the kids must be hurt, but that's the way it is these days. When Eric is grown up, he will no doubt have lots of happy memories of his father. Fred and Ingrid may be jealous of all that attention they never had, but at least he is finally paying some attention to them. But they're adults now. Somehow, it doesn't seem the same. In a rare moment of candour with a reporter, Lightfoot asked, "Did you ever have your son look at you with accusation that you walked out on him?" There are still many hurts from the past that need to be rectified.

All the old, troubled relationships seem to have settled into familiarity. Lightfoot will say he's "on friendly terms with everyone" now. There are still old wounds that ache, though, in everybody's bones. While everybody involved seems to have come to terms with their history, Brita and Smith and Coonley have all had psychiatric therapy to help them arrive at where they are today. Not Lightfoot. His songs are his psychotherapy.

He spent the first half of 1988 in the Eastern Sound Studios of Toronto recording his newest album, *Gord's Gold, Volume II*. It is the second summing-up of his music during his career. He has re-recorded his best songs of the past thirteen years. It has a bright, punchy sound achieved by recording live with his current band—Terry Clements on guitar, Rick Haynes on bass, Barry Keane on drums and Mike Heffernan on keyboard—on the recording studio floor. It is, in a way, a return to an older recording technique, before producers and knob-twirlers and light-emitting devices gutted the heart and soul from records, back to the days when songwriters and singers and engineers were forced to rely on instinct and imagination to create a hit record, to a time before click tracks and tape loops and synthesized sounds dictated the meaning of a record.

Nobody will think of *Gord's Gold, Volume II* as a major creative breakthrough. But, still, it is nice to hear "Alberta Bound" and "Wreck of the Edmund Fitzgerald" and "Cherokee Bend" and fifteen other of his best songs of the last thirteen years all on one album, all done with care and with feeling.

And maybe that will be the end of his writing and of his recording career. Lightfoot never seemed to like the recording studio anyway. He once compared making a new record to going to the dentist. He doesn't know if he's got any more songs left in him. He says he'd rather just tour around from city to city and forget about writing and recording. For a while, at least. Maybe he will go that route. Who knows?

Other pop musicians renew their creativity by seeking out new musicians, new styles of music, new producers. Working with David Foster didn't seem to be the way to go, but maybe somewhere there's some young hot-shot musicians who'd love to work with Lightfoot, maybe somewhere there's a producer who can hear inside of him exactly how he would produce Lightfoot to make him fresh and new again. Maybe it will happen. Maybe not.

If the music seems so familiar, perhaps it is because he has made twenty albums over the years. He could probably do with a rest, and a change in direction someday. You get the feeling, though, that a change in direction is impossible now. Maybe you don't hear about Lightfoot as you used to do years ago, but to assume he's retired would be fanciful. A slowing down, perhaps. He still makes a lot of appearances on tour. He joined the Canadian pop star effort, Northern Lights for Africa, to raise funds to aid the starving people of Ethiopia with the song "Tears Are Not Enough." Everybody who is anybody in Canadian pop music is on that song: Joni Mitchell, Neil Young, David Foster, Bryan Adams. It is Lightfoot who starts the song off, catching your ear with the first verse. The record raised a lot of money and made everybody feel good, almost like it was the sixties all over again and people could join together for the joy of singing and to help the weak and the helpless.

That was him on your television at the opening festivities of the Calgary Olympics, along with Ian Tyson, singing Lightfoot's song, "Alberta Bound" and Tyson's "Four Strong Winds." It had that good, old-timey feeling, although you couldn't help but feel that all our past is contained in Lightfoot and Tyson, and the future might be in another singer who appeared on that show, K.D. Lang.

In concert at Massey Hall, 1987. (Photo by Fred Thornhill, courtesy of Lightfoot)

With Ian Tyson, preparing for the opening ceremonies of the 1988 Olympic games in Calgary.

So you see, he's not really retired, he just doesn't get around
as much as he used to.

Maybe it's just that it's not the old days anymore. His
favourite sports team, the Toronto Maple Leafs, are a sad,
bedraggled band of losers these days, an embarrassment to
their home town. The Pilot Tavern has moved a few streets
away from where it used to be; it's not a hangout for artists
and intellectuals anymore, it appeals to secretaries celebrating birthdays and to couples about to hone in on each other
in sexual embrace. Not only the Riverboat but all of
Yorkville has gone, the music and the ideas and the colour
replaced by boutiques, lawyers and Mercedes Benzes. Yes,
that must be it, it's just not the same old days anymore.

There is one Toronto landmark that hasn't changed,
though. On the corner of Schuter and Victoria Streets, near
its newer neighbour, The Eaton Centre, Massey Hall still
stands in squat brick ugliness, its pattern of fire escapes
telling us perhaps more than we care to know about
management's fear of fire. Despite its ugliness, the nine-
teenth-century building has seen a lot of good music over
the years.

It's been more than thirty years since Lightfoot the child
first sang at Massey Hall. He's sung there each year for the
past two decades and he'll no doubt sing there again. Bernie
Fiedler will produce the show, and it will make a ton of
money. Fiedler and Lightfoot, the two "cronies," go back a
long way together. Fiedler has made Lightfoot a lot of
money. But when Fiedler was in trouble with the tax department, it was Lightfoot who paid a small fortune to bail him
out. And it was through Fiedler that Lightfoot met Cathy
Smith, Cathy Coonley and Elizabeth Moon. Together, they
will no doubt triumph at Massey Hall once again.

Maple Leafs fans still jam Maple Leaf Gardens to see the
sad hockey team which once was the pride of the city. They
live on past glory and future hope. Lightfoot's fans still fill

Massey Hall every year, but it's different for them. The past and the present and the future are all one for Lightfoot's fans. They have a pact with Lightfoot stronger than marriage vows or a written contract. For as ever long as he will sing to them, they will listen to him. It is a pact unique in show business, a handshake deal that will endure as long as there is still a song left inside of Lightfoot. When Lightfoot steps out onto that Massey Hall stage, it is a validation of all our youth.

The intense excitement is gone now, gone both from Lightfoot and from his audience. Familiar comfort has replaced it. At the end of the Massey Hall concerts, there are no more nine-day parties. Lightfoot is sober twenty-four hours of every day. The wild passions are gone now, replaced by the comfort of his money and his mansion.

Lightfoot is now turning some of his passion and lots of his money into environmental concerns. He is working with scientist David Suzuki on a project to save part of the forests of British Columbia from the loggers' saws and has a long-term plan to help fight the depletion of the earth's ozone layer. These projects will probably provide him with long-term satisfactions, but will never replace the adrenalin rush of facing a stomping, clapping, cheering audience.

There's a portrait Robert Markle did of Lightfoot a long time ago. It's all colours and swirling lines: a representation of power, energy and talent, a graphic depiction of a whirling dervish churning through life at a pace no one else could maintain.

If Markle were to do a new portrait, it would be different. The canvas might consist mostly of emptiness, with a tiny figure over in one corner. The tiny figure might still represent power and energy, but it might also indicate tiredness and satisfaction that now Lightfoot has everything and can afford to be nice to everyone. Markle might put a smile on the face of the figure.

Or else, he might paint Lightfoot as an Old Testament prophet, one of those prophets who—no matter the details of his own personal life—has been given the responsibility and the duty to tell us all what is required of us in this life. Perhaps the prophet would be bellowing to us from the mountain-top, and it would be clear that we are not listening. Perhaps the prophet would be warning us that we must take lessons from our national history; or he would be detailing the pleasures of unconditional love and the pain of false love, or warning us of the wrath of nature when her hospitality has been abused; or else he may be simply telling us what it is like to be one man who lives in Canada at this time. Perhaps it is the pain of knowing that people do not really listen, except in the most superficial manner, to prophets disguised as pop singers—just ask Bob Dylan about that—that has led Lightfoot down the paths he has chosen in his lifetime.

Lots of people claim they can read Lightfoot's mind. They will direct you: go back to Orillia, his life is clear if you understand Orillia; listen to the lyrics he was written, it's all laid out there. Like Rosicrucians or Pyramidists, many people tell you there is a secret to his psyche that, if unlocked, will reveal to you everything you need to know about Gordon Meredith Lightfoot. They are only partly right, of course: all these things contribute a little to understanding his personality, but there really is no Rosetta Stone available to decipher his mind.

And yet, late at night, if you put on an old Lightfoot album and you listen to "Song For a Winter Night" or "Don Quixote" or "A Minor Ballad," you can easily remember what was so young, so golden, in all our past.

Perhaps, late at night, in the mansion on the quiet millionaire street, Lightfoot plays one of the old albums, and perhaps he, too, remembers. He might remember all the self-images of his youth: as a ghost in a wishing well with

(Photo by Boris Spremo, courtesy of the Toronto *Star*).

chains upon his feet; as Don Quixote riding the countryside, lance in hand; as a traveller in the early morning rain,
a suitcase in his hand; as a young stranger greeted by his
mother at her kitchen table; as the ship captain sailing the
Sea of Tranquility.

Perhaps.

If he does, he knows—as do we all—that in the end it is
the music that matters. If you could read his mind you
would find all the ghosts of shipwrecks and old lovers and
old friends and old songs. Late at night, just listen to the old
songs.

Index

Discography

1988	*Gord's Gold Volume II*	Warner Bros.	(Sept. 1988)
1986	*East Of Midnight*	Warner Bros.	25482
1983	*Salute*	Warner Bros.	1-23901
1982	*Shadows*	Warner Bros.	BSK 3633
1980	*Dream Street Rose*	Warner Bros.	XHS 3426
1978	*Endless Wire*	Warner Bros.	KBS 3149
1976	*Summertime Dream*	Reprise	MS 2246
1975	*Gord's Gold*	Reprise	2RX 2237
1975	*Cold On The Shoulder*	Reprise	MS 2206
1974	*Sundown*	Reprise	MS 2177
1972	*Old Dan's Records*	Reprise	MS 2116
1972	*Don Quixote*	Reprise	MS 2056
1971	*Summer Side Of Life*	Reprise	MS 2037
1970	*Sit Down Young Stranger (If You Could Read My Mind)*	Reprise	RS 6392
1969	*Sunday Concert*	United Artists	UAS 6714
1968	*Back Here On Earth*	United Artists	UAS 6672
1968	*Did She Mention My Name*	United Artists	UAS 6649
1967	*The Way I Feel*	United Artists	UAS 6587
1965	*Lightfoot*	United Artists	UAS 6487
1962	*Two Tones At The Village Corner*	Chateau	CLP 1012